A WAY OUT OF ETH...

(Untangling the Values Fiasco in North America)

by
Earle F. Zeigler
Ph.D., LL.D., D.Sc.

Trafford Publishing

2004

© Copyright 2004 Earle F. Zeigler Ph.D., LL.D., D.Sc. All rights reserved.

No part of this publication may be reproduced, stored in a retrieval system, or transmitted, in any form or by any means, electronic, mechanical, photocopying, recording, or otherwise, without the written prior permission of the author.

Printed in Victoria, Canada

Note for Librarians: a cataloguing record for this book that includes Dewey Classification and US Library of Congress numbers is available from the National Library of Canada. The complete cataloguing record can be obtained from the National Library's online database at: www.nlc-bnc.ca/amicus/index-e.html
ISBN 1-4120-2274-6

TRAFFORD

This book was published *on-demand* **in cooperation with Trafford Publishing.**
On-demand publishing is a unique process and service of making a book available for retail sale to the public taking advantage of on-demand manufacturing and Internet marketing. **On-demand publishing** includes promotions, retail sales, manufacturing, order fulfilment, accounting and collecting royalties on behalf of the author.

Suite 6E, 2333 Government St., Victoria, B.C. V8T 4P4, CANADA
Phone   250-383-6864   Toll-free   1-888-232-4444 (Canada & US)
Fax   250-383-6804   E-mail   sales@trafford.com
Web site   www.trafford.com
TRAFFORD PUBLISHING IS A DIVISION OF TRAFFORD HOLDINGS LTD.
Trafford Catalogue #04-0102   www.trafford.com/robots/04-0102.html

10   9   8   7   6   5   4   3

DEDICATION

I dedicate this book to those people
who helped me arrive at my present position
about human values and their overriding importance
for the individual and for the society.

I believe there is an urgent need to challenge
the underlying human values and norms that have determined
the direction in which the United States is heading
in the 21st Century.

CONCEPTUAL INDEX

Dedication	iii
Conceptual Index	v
Preface	viii

Section		**Page**
Section One	AN EMERGING POSTMODERN AGE	1
	Significant Developments Have Transformed Our Lives	2
	The World Has Three Major Trading Blocks	3
	The Impact of Negative Social Forces Has Increased	5
	The Problems of Megalopolis Living Have Not Yet Been Solved	5
	What Character Do We Seek for People?	6
	What Happened to the Original Enlightenment Ideal?	7
	Technology and Life Improvement	8
	Postmodernism as an Influence	9
Section Two	THE ETHICAL DECISION-MAKING DILEMMA	12
	Ethical Decision-Making	13
	No Universal Ethical Foundation Available	14
	An Elementary Approach to Ethics	16
	The Young Person's Sense of Life	18
	Summary	19
Section Three	FROM PERSONAL TO PROFESSIONAL TO ENVIRONMENTAL ETHICS	20
	Rapid Change Brings Ethical Confusion	20
	Impending Cultural Clashes	22
	Values of a Liberal Society	22
	The Professions: Yesterday and Today	24
	A Plan for the Future	26

What Are the Major "Routes" for Ethical Decision-Making Available?		29
1. Authoritarianism (Legalism)		32
2. Relativism (Antinomianism)		33
3. Situationism		34
4. Scientific Ethics		35
5. The "Good Reasons" Approach		36
6. Emotivism		38
Table 1: Comparative Aspects of Major Philosophical Approaches to Ethical Decision-Making (Part 1)		39
Table 2: Comparative Aspects of Major Philosophical Approaches to Ethical Decision-Making (Part 2)		40
Summary		41

Section Four EMERGING FROM ETHICAL CONFUSION 45

The First Half of the 20th Century 45
The Second Half of the 20th Century 46
Three Philosophers: 50
   Kant's Test of Consistency (Step 1) 51
   Mill's Test of (Net) Consequences (Step 2) 52
   Aristotle's Test of Intentions (Step 3) 54
Developing a Legal Argument to Back Up the
   Three-Step Plan 56
Summary 64

Section Five EXAMPLES OF THE THREE-STEP APPROACH TO ETHICAL DECISION-MAKING 66

Personal Ethical Decision-Making Problems 66
  Introduction
  Case 1: "Beth's & Tim's Dilemma" 67
  Case 2: "Having It Both Ways" 70
Professional Ethical Decision-Making Problems 73
  Introduction
  Case 1: "Everybody's Doin' It" 78
  Case 2: "Is the 'Climate' Better Down South?" 81
Environmental Ethical Decision-Making Problems 84
  Introduction

	Case 1: "Shall I Run for Elective Office?"	86
	Case 2: "The Right to Bear Arms"	89
	Table 15: Sample Form for Use With Analyses	92

Section Six SCIENTIFIC ETHICS: A REOMMENDATION
FOR THE LONG-TERM   94

    Brief historical background   94
    A person's implicit sense of life   96
    The selection of one from among several
       approaches to ethical decision-making   97
    Employing a pragmatic, scientific-method
       approach to ethical decision-making   97
    An Example of a Practical Application: 101
      (Application of a scientific approach to the
      professional/semiprofessional/amateur
      controversy)
    Summary   105

Section Seven THE FUTURE   107

    How We Might Improve the Planet   107
    Achieving a "Scotch Verdict" about the Future   111
    A Final "Playback"   115

References & Bibliography   117

Preface

This book was written because I found myself terribly upset about the direction in which the world is heading. Because I am in the midst of North America as a dual citizen, I feel sad that we here appear to be a large part of the world's problem! I had thought it would be a better place for all people by the year 2000. Because it doesn't seem to be heading in that direction, I am forced to conclude (1) that in many ways we are confused about what our values are at the present, (2) that we need to reconsider them and then *re-state* exactly what we believe they are in light of the changing times, and (3) finally that we will then need to assess more carefully--*on a regular basis*--whether we are living up to those values we have chosen and so often glibly espouse.

Although well into my 85th year--and obviously will not be around forever--I am especially disturbed about what is happening in the U.S.A. I believe that the world's only superpower is (and has been!) playing a very negative role with its international efforts over the years--as well-intentioned as it claims they are and may indeed be in particular instances. At the same time I also believe that the States has been disintegrating *within* from the standpoint of human values. I just happen to have been born as a citizen of the country that was once supposed to be "the last best hope on earth." Now the "last best hope" is that the rest of the world through the power and influence of a *sound* United Nations will somehow be able to persuade the United States to fulfill its avowed purposes *and stay in its proper place.*

Born in 1919 at the end of World War I in Queens, a borough of New York City, I grew up there in what was subsequently viewed as the "roaring twenties." This presumed uproar and bedlam did not affect me, however. Through the devoted efforts of my grandparents and working mother, I eventually learned a bit more than on which side to butter toast. My mother had divorced my father when I was two years old (a significant "fracture" in those times). She subsequently married again, to a Baptist minister, and we three moved to South Norwalk, CT. At 12 years of age I had acquired a stepfather and, in a minor way, I suppose you could say that was the beginning of my "time of troubles." I must say that I was quite probably a "handful," and that he did his best to cope with me. However, we never were on quite the same wave length, a fact that actually helped me decide where I stood on many aspects of life. I should be thankful because such a relationship while an adolescent--as the minister's son(!), coupled with the developing social and political scene of the 1930s and 1940s, did much to shape my future orientation to the world around me.

I live in Canada now, and eventually became a citizen here too after moving here for the second time. Thus, I pay taxes in both countries. Frankly, as a sort of "refugee" I live here because I like the climate better. That statement undoubtedly sounds a bit odd because Canada is said to be "the land of ice, snow, Indians, and people who speak French," However, I live in the lower mainland of British Columbia where that white stuff is a distinct rarity. It does rain more than occasionally, I must admit. And in BC alone, we have 100 native Indian tribes (now known as nations) that are distributed geographically throughout the province. I keep telling my grandson that he'd be better off eventually living somewhere else than here. Why? Because only one land claim by one aboriginal tribe (nation!) has been settled by the province. After the other 99 settlements are consummated, there won't be any room for the rest of BC's multi-ethnic population to sit down. Finally, although the speaking of French is promoted quite vigorously, way out here on the West Coast one might be better advised to learn Mandarin (Chinese)!

More seriously, when I said above that I liked the climate in Canada better, that was a play on words too. What I really meant was that presently I find Canada a country in which my present beliefs and social philosophy fit much better than they did in the U.S.A. as presently constituted. I have done very well in my field over a period of 60+ years divided equally between both countries. Therefore, I can say that moving back and forth between the two countries was actually not a question of my liking periodically to be "a bigger fish in a smaller pond." (Canada's population of 30 million or so is only that of the State of California.) To come to the point, there are now so many aspects about the

U.S. that turn me off that I hardly know where to begin in explaining my position.

For example, I am very upset about the fact that the United States became the first country in the 21st century to defy the United Nations by waging war against Iraq ostensibly to oust an evil dictator. I know that he was a tyrant who oversaw many terrible acts by his sons and other henchmen. But that's not the point. The U.S. has set a terrible precedent in a highly troubled world by its action. (I must point out that Canada did not approve this almost unilateral action.) And what or who is next? My television set has just announced that George "W" is going to step up the United States' long-standing effort to oust Castro. Egad! "Who's next" in the parade of countries the U.S. is determined to democratize (or whatever!) while exporting capitalism, technology, and Christianity as well?

For a second example of the prevailing climate that disturbs me in the United States, let me move to an area where I worked professionally for another example. Having taught, administered, and periodically coached sport at Yale, Michigan, and Illinois, I can speak more authoritatively about sport in general and more specifically about intercollegiate athletics in the States. Sport in the Ivy League and similar institutions (Division 3, NCAA) is typically fine. It's doing quite well what it's intended to do. But athletics in those universities where gate receipts is a vital factor has gradually but steadily throughout the entire 20th century gotten completely out of hand. It is semi-professional, and this fact has somehow occasioned all of the attendant vices that somehow have crept into such programs when sponsored by educational institutions.

This most unfortunate development throughout the 20th century is only symptomatic of the entire society, however. My position in this realm of society is basically this: "Sport was created by humans to serve humans beneficially." As it seems to be now, many professional and semi-professional athletes--not to mention the situation in overly emphasized high school sport competition--are there to serve what has become a most undesirable "sport goliath." It is accompanied and insidiously goaded by a mindless public watching with vicarious, often rapturous involvement. All of this is akin to the seduction of the populace that occurred in ancient Rome. Sadly, while this is taking place, the overwhelming majority of children and young people is getting a poor (or no!) introduction to what ought to be a a fine program of health instruction, physical activity education, and physical recreation in the public schools and related institutions. Not only are "the rich getting richer, and the poor poorer," the elite athletes are getting the attention, and the normal and challenged youngsters are getting fatter!

What this boils down to is that--almost everywhere one turns--there is a crisis in human values as we move into the 21st century. This has created what I call an ethical decision-making dilemma. In recent books, *Who Knows What's Right Anymore?* and *Whatever Happened to "the Good Life?"*, both published by Trafford in 2002, I strove to get to the heart of this massive problem in different ways. Here I argue again that, for several reasons, the child and adolescent in society today are missing out almost completely on a sound "experiential" introduction to ethics. This is true whether we are referring to what takes place in the home, the school system, or the church--actually an experience that occurs inadequately--*if at all!* In fact, the truth is that typically no systematic instruction in this most important subject is offered at any time. (And I refuse to accept the often-heard "osmosis stance"--that such knowledge is "better caught than taught.") Granted that it helps to have people around you who are setting good examples. However, in the final analysis it's the individual who makes judgments and decisions based on experiences undergone.

Initially I will explain how this all came about, how and why such a terrible gap exists. Previously, for many, at least a relatively strong, orthodox, religious indoctrination prevailed--whether a person followed such strictures or not. Today I believe such indoctrination as exists is most inadequate, is steadily declining, and really doesn't "fill the bill" either. This is not necessarily a bad thing in one respect. because these institutions have not kept up with the times because of the built-in rigidity of their doctrines. *(If they don't adjust, they should be replaced!)* Moreover, the situation has steadily changed in our present multi-ethnic, secular culture to a point where "confusion reigns" as to ethical conduct of either a personal, professional, or environmental nature.

My objective in **Section One** is to assess the North American situation in what has been called the postmodern age. I believe that Americans, and many Canadians as well, do not fully comprehend their unique position in the history of the world's development. In all probability this status will change radically as the 21st century progresses. For that matter, I believe that the years ahead are going to be really difficult and trying for the large majority of the world's citizens. Basically, however, the United States, as the one major nuclear power, has deliberately assumed the ongoing, overriding task of maintaining large-scale peace. This will be increasingly difficult because a variety of countries, both large and small, may already have, or may soon have, nuclear-arms capability. That is one stark fact that makes the future so worrisome.

Section One has provided a background for the remainder of the book by discussing the North American situation in the postmodern age. Then, in **Section Two**, there is an explanation of the "ethical gap" that exists insofar as people's understanding of ethical decision-making in relation to society's values and norms.

Following this, in **Section Three**, I will explain how we are called upon ***daily*** for ethical opinions and/or decisions about *personal,* or *professional,* or *environmental (social)* problems. In this connection I believe that a person's ethical involvement should be an implicit/experiential approach that typically move daily from one to the other of the three categories mentioned (e.g., personal). At this point, mostly in chart form, I offer a quick look at six of the major ethical routes or approaches extant as offered by the discipline of philosophy. These "guides," if followed carefully--that is, one or the other--lead to solutions to many of the problems that prevail in today's confusing Western-world scenario. Interestingly, and disturbingly, however, one would be hard pressed to find a friend or colleague who consciously has chosen or understands one or another of these approaches to ethical decision-making.

I have observed that most books of this nature recommend what amounts to ***one*** specific philosophical, religious, or common-sense source. In this regard I believe fervently that the reader must ultimately make his or her own personal decision about which approach to follow--if any! However, if or when it does happen, I hope it will be one that is determined by the individual when the "age of reason" is achieved (let us say, after age 13).

I decided therefore to offer an "easy-entry" approach in **Section Four**, a three-step one that can be used safely before a person makes a final decision as to which ethical decision-making approach to follow as more experience and maturation occurs during life. Admittedly, many may never proceed beyond this initial (three-step) stage--if they get this far! Incidentally, this three-step approach recommended can also be checked or vetted to a degree by seeking to "equate" it with a jurisprudential (law-court) analysis of the ethical decision to be made. And, fortunately, most of us hear or see or read about law-court trials daily and understand the process quite well.

In **Section Five**, after brief explanations of each type of dilemma faced, respectively, when confronted with personal, or professional, or social/environmental problems daily, I offer two examples of each using the three-step approach to resolve such decision-making problems. I then decided also that I had a basic responsibility to make my own position on ethical decision-making known clearly. In the turbulent 1960s most students demanded this as a right--that is, something that their instructor *owed* to them. Today I personally believe that has been called "scientific ethics" offers the best hope for the entire world in the 21st century. (This is one of the positions discussed briefly earlier in decision-making approach IV on p. 38.) So, in **Section VI,** I explain why I have personally accepted this approach for use immediately after I have carried out the ***initial*** three-step scanning of the situation at hand. (I must explain, however, that definitive scientific evidence about this or that problem is often not readily available when needed.)

Lastly, in **Section VII**, I suggest an approach to "looking to the future," a future about which we should all be very concerned. In addition to being worried about simply the *presence* of human life on Earth, I am worried about the status of individual freedom in our lives. I say this being reminded of Muller's concept of the "tragic sense" of life. We need to improve the planet Earth in so many ways.

I want to express my ongoing appreciation and gratitude to those who have helped me. The folks at Trafford, especially Ben Harrison and Terry Lussier, were most helpful and patient in moving this project along and in getting material formatted properly for Trafford's online, on-demand printing service. As in my previous trade books, I am most appreciative of the help (the interesting covers!) and advice received from Andy Naval of Accugraphics Ltd. in Richmond.

Finally, I have found this to be a fascinating area for study, reflection, and ethical practice. We all need to understand the world situation and the North American scene as fully as possible. To the greatest extent possible, we simply must rely on incontrovertible scientific evidence and applied ethics to help us improve our ethical decision-making. It is my most sincere hope that you will find at least some of these ideas and thoughts, and one of these approaches to analysis, helpful as you face the ever-present, changing ethical problems that will confront you in the years ahead.

Earle F. Zeigler, Richmond, BC, Canada, 2004

PREAMBLE

Today's world is incredibly complicated. This is why it is vital that we search for better approaches to living--"**flow experiences**"--that will "improve its quality and lead to more joyful and fruitful involvement." In the process "the growth and liberation of the self" should be combined " with that of society as a whole" (Csikszentmihalyi, 1993, p. 5).

Some people include flow experiences in their life patterns, and thereby improve their quality of life. If some can do this, many more people should have this opportunity (i.e., the freedom to do so) in the future. Before this can happen, doubters must be convinced of the possibility and desirability of adding such experiences to their lives. This leads to the perennial question in education: What knowledge, competencies, character, and personality traits should we educate for in the years ahead?

Such choices are necessarily based on the values and norms of the culture in which people live. Values are the major social forces that help to determine the direction a culture will take at any given moment. Such values as social values, educational values, scientific values, artistic values, etc. make up the highest level of the social system in a culture. These values represent the "ideal general character" (e.g., social-structured facilitation of individual achievement, equality of opportunity). Remember that overall culture in itself also serves a "pattern-maintenance function" as a society confronts the ongoing functional problems it faces.

Further, the values people hold have a direct relationship to how the nature of the human being is conceived. A number of attempts have been made to define human nature on a rough historical time scale. For example, the human has been conceived in five different ways in historical progression as (1) a rational animal, (2) a spiritual being, (3) a receptacle of knowledge, (4) a mind that can be trained by exercise, and (5) a problem-solving organism (Morris, 1956). Likewise, Berelson and Steiner (1964) traced six behavioral-science images of man and woman throughout recorded history. These were identified chronologically as the (1) a philosophical image, (2) a Christian image, (3) a political image, (4) an economic image, (5) a psychoanalytic image, and (6) a behavioral-science image.

Whatever one decides about his or her basic nature (e.g., problem-solving organism with a behavioral science image), a mature person will eventually decide what constitutes "the good life." This is why education for "value determination" is so basic in the educational process.

SECTION I
An Emerging Postmodern Age

North Americans do not fully comprehend that their unique position in the history of the world's development will in all probability change radically in the 21st century. For that matter. the years ahead are really going to be difficult ones for all of the world's citizens. The United States, as the one major nuclear power, has assumed the ongoing, massive problem of maintaining large-scale peace. Of course, a variety of countries, both large and small, may or may not have nuclear arms capability as well. That is what is so worrisome.

Additionally, all of the world will be having increasingly severe ecological problems, not to mention the ebbs and flows of an energy crisis. Generally, also, there is a worldwide nutritional problem, as well as an ongoing situation where the rising expectations of the underdeveloped nations, including their staggering debt (and ours!), will somehow have to be met. These are just a few of the major concerns looming on the horizon.

Indeed, although it is seemingly more true of the United States than Canada, history is going against Americans in several ways. This means that their previous optimism must be tempered to shake them loose from delusions they have acquired.. For example, despite the presence of the United Nations, the United States has persisted in envisioning itself--as the world superpower--as almost being endowed by the Creator to make all crucial political decisions. Such decisions, often to act unilaterally with the hoped-for, but belated sanction of the United Nations, have resulted in United States-led incursions in the Middle East in the two wars and into Somalia for very different reasons. And there are other similar situations that are now history (e.g., Cuba Afghanistan, the former Yugoslavia, Rwanda, Sudan, Haiti, etc., respectively, not to mention other suspected incursions).

Nevertheless, there is reason to expect selected U.S. retrenchment brought on by its excessive world involvement and enormous debt. Of course, any such retrenchment would inevitably lead to a decline in the economic and military influence of the United States. But who can argue logically that the present uneasy balance of power is a healthy situation looking to the future? Norman Cousins appeared to have sounded just the right note more than a generation ago when he stated that "the most important factor in the complex equation of the future is the way the human mind responds to crisis" (1974, 6-7). The world culture as we know it must respond adequately to the many challenges with which it is being confronted. The societies and nations must individually and collectively respond positively, intelligently, and strongly if humanity as we have known it is to survive.

Significant Developments Have "Transformed Our Lives"

In this discussion of national and international developments, with an eye to achieving some historical perspective on the subject, we should also keep in mind the specific developments in the last quarter of the 20th century. For example, Naisbitt (1982) outlined the "ten new directions that are transforming our lives," as well as the "megatrends" insofar as women's evolving role in societal structure (Aburdene & Naisbitt, 1992). Here I am referring to:

(1) the concepts of the information society and the Internet,
(2) "high tech/high touch,"
(3) the shift to world economy,
(4) the need to shift to long-term thinking in regard to ecology,
(5) the move toward organizational decentralization,
(6) the trend toward self-help,
(7) the ongoing discussion of the wisdom of participatory democracy as opposed to representative democracy,
(8) a shift toward networking,
(9) a reconsideration of the "north-south" orientation, and
(10) the viewing of decisions as "multiple option" instead of "either/or."

Add to this the ever-increasing, lifelong involvement of women in the workplace, politics, sports, organized religion, and social activism, Now we begin to understand that a new world order has descended upon us as we begin the 21st century.

Moving ahead in time slightly beyond Naisbitt's first set of Megatrends, a second list of 10 issues facing political leaders was highlighted as "Ten events that shook the world between 1984 and 1994" (*Utne Reader,* 1994, pp. 58-74). Consider the following:

(1) the fall of communism and the continuing rise of nationalism,
(2) the environmental crisis and the Green movement,
(3) the AIDS epidemic and the "gay response,"
(4) continuing wars and the peace movement,
(5) the gender war,
(6) religion and racial tension,
(7) the concept of "West meets East" and resultant implications,
(8) the "Baby Boomers" came of age and "Generation X" has started to worry and complain because of declining expectation levels,
(9) the whole idea of globalism and international markets, and
(10) the computer revolution and the specter of Internet.

The World Has Three Major Trading Blocks

Concurrent with the above developments, to help cope with such change the world's "economic manageability" may have been helped by its division into three major trading blocs: (1) the Pacific Rim dominated by Japan, (2) the European Community very heavily influenced by Germany, and (3) North America dominated by the United States of America. While this appears to be true to some observers, interestingly perhaps something even more fundamental has occurred. Succinctly put, world politics seems to be "entering a new phase in which the fundamental source of conflict will be neither ideological nor economic." In the place of these, Samuel P. Huntington, of Harvard's Institute for Strategic Studies, believes that now the major conflicts in the world will actually be clashes between different groups of civilizations espousing fundamentally different cultures (*The New York Times*, June 6, 1993, E19).

These clashes, Huntington states, represent a distinct shift away from viewing the world as being composed of first, second, and third worlds as was the case during the cold war. Thus, Huntington is arguing that in the 21st century the world will return to a pattern of development evident several hundred years ago in which civilizations will actually rise and fall. (Interestingly, this is exactly what was postulated by the late Arnold Toynbee in his earlier famous theory of history development.)

Thus, internationally, with the dissolution of the Union of Soviet Socialist Republics (USSR), Russia and the remaining communist regimes are being severely challenged as they seek to convert to more of a capitalistic economic system. Additionally, a number of other multinational countries have either broken up, or are showing signs of potential breakups (e.g., Yugoslavia, China, Canada). Further, the evidence points to the strong possibility that the developing nations are becoming ever poorer and more destitute with burgeoning populations and widespread starvation setting in.

Further, Western Europe is facing a demographic time bomb even more than the United States because of the influx of refugees from African and Islamic countries, not to mention refugees from countries of the former Soviet Union. It appears further that the European Community will be inclined to appease Islam's demands. However, the multinational nature of the European Community will tend to bring on economic protectionism to insulate its economy against the rising costs of prevailing socialist legislation.

Still further, there is some evidence that Radical Islam, along with Communist China, may well become increasingly aggressive toward the Western culture of Europe and North America. At present, Islam gives evidence of replacing Marxism as the world's main ideology of confrontation. For example, Islam is dedicated to regaining control of Jerusalem and to force Israel to give up control of land occupied earlier to provide a buffer zone against Arab aggressors. (Also, China has been arming certain Arab nations. But how can we be too critical in this regard when we recall that the U.S.A. has also armed selected countries in the past [and present?] when such support was deemed in its interest?)

As Hong Kong is absorbed into Communist China, further political problems seem inevitable in the Far East as well. Although North Korea is facing agricultural problems, there is the possibility (probability?) of the building of nuclear bombs there. (Further, there is the ever-present fear worldwide that small nations and terrorists will somehow get nuclear weapons too.) A growing Japanese assertiveness in Asian and world affairs also seems inevitable because of its typically very strong financial position. Yet the flow of foreign capital from Japan into North America has slowed down somewhat because Japan is being confronted with its own financial crisis caused by inflated real estate and market values. There would obviously be a strong reaction to any fall in living standards in this tightly knit society. Interestingly, still further, the famed Japanese work ethic has become somewhat tarnished by the growing attraction of leisure opportunities.

The situation in Africa has become increasingly grim because the countries south of the Sahara

Desert (that is, the dividing line between black Africa and the Arab world) experienced extremely bad economic performance in the past two decades). This social influence has brought to a halt much of the continental effort leading to political liberalization while at the same time exacerbating traditional ethnic rivalries. This economic problem has accordingly forced governmental cutbacks in many of the countries because of the pressures brought to bear by the financial institutions of the Western world that have been underwriting much of the development. The poor are therefore getting poorer, and health (AIDs!) and education standards have in many instances deteriorated even lower than they were previously.

The Impact of Negative Social Forces Has Increased.

Now, shifting the focus of this discussion from the problems of an unsettled "Global Village" back to the problem of "living the good life" in the 21st century in North America, we are finding that the human recreational experience will have to be earned typically within a society whose very structure has been modified. For example, (1) the concept of the traditional family structure has been strongly challenged by a variety of social forces (e.g., economics, divorce rate); (2) many single people are finding that they must work longer hours; and (3) many families need more than one breadwinner just to make ends meet. Also, the idea of a steady surplus economy may have vanished, temporarily it is hoped, in the presence of a substantive drive to reduce a budgetary deficit by introducing major cutbacks in so-called nonessentials.

The Problems of Megalopolis Living Have Not Yet Been Solved

Additionally, many of the same problems of megalopolis living described as early as the 1960s still prevail and are even increasing (e.g., declining infrastructure, rising crime rates, transportation gridlocks, overcrowded schools). Interestingly, in that same year of 1967, Prime Minister Lester Pearson asked Canadians to improve "the quality of Canadian life" as Canada celebrated her 100th anniversary as a confederation. And still today, despite all of Canada's current identity problems, she can take some pride in the fact that Canada has on occasion been proclaimed as the best place on earth to live (with the United States not very far behind). Nevertheless, we can't escape the fact that the work week is not getting shorter and shorter. Also, Michael's prediction about four different types of leisure class still seems a distant dream for the large majority of people.

Further, the situation has developed in such a way that the presently maturing generation, so-called Generation X, is finding that fewer good-paying jobs are available and the average annual income is declining (especially if we keep a steadily rising cost of living in mind). What caused this to happen? This is not a simple question to answer. For one thing, despite the rosy picture envisioned a generation ago, one in which we were supposedly entering a new stage for humankind, we are unable today to cope adequately with the multitude of problems that have developed. This situation is true whether inner city, suburbia, exurbia, or small-town living are concerned. Transportation jams and gridlock, for example, are occurring daily as public transportation struggles to meet rising demand for economical transport within the framework of developing megalopolises.

Certainly, megalopolis living trends have not abated and will probably not do so in the predictable future. More and more families, where that unit is still present, need two breadwinners just to survive. Interest rates, although minor cuts are made when economic slowdowns occur, remain quite high. This discourages many people from home ownership. Pollution of air and water continues despite efforts of many to change the present course of development. High-wage industries seem to be "heading south" in search of places where lower wages can be paid. Also, all sorts of crime are still present in our society, a goodly portion of it seemingly brought about by unemployment and rising debt at all levels from the individual to the federal government. The rise in youth crime is especially disturbing. In this respect, it is fortunate in North America that municipal, private-agency, and public recreation has received continuing financial support from the increasingly burdened taxpayer. Even here, however, there has been a definite trend toward user fees for many services.

What Character Do We Seek for People?

Still further, functioning in a world that is steadily becoming a "Global Village," we need to think more seriously than ever before about the character and traits for which we should seek to develop in people. The so-called developed nations can only continue to lead or strive for the proverbial good life if children and young people develop the right attitudes (psychologically speaking) toward (1) education, (2) work, (3) (use of leisure), (4) participation in government, (5) various types of consumption, and (6) concern for world stability and peace. Make no mistake about it. If we truly desire "the good life," education for the creative and constructive use of leisure--as a significant part of ongoing general education--should have a unique role to play from here on into the indeterminate future.

What are called the Old World countries all seem to have a "character." It is almost something that they take for granted. However, it is questionable whether there is anything that can be called a character in North America (i.e., in the United States, in Canada). Americans were thought earlier to be heterogeneous and individualistic as a people, as opposed to Canadians. But the Canadian culture--whatever that may be today!--has changed quite a bit in recent decades toward multiculturalism--not to mention French-speaking Quebec, of course--as people arrived from many different lands. (Of course, Canada was founded by two distinct cultures, the English and the French.)

Shortly after the middle of the twentieth century, Commager (1966), the noted historian, enumerated what he believed were some common denominators in American (i.e., U.S.) character. These, he said, were (1) carelessness; (2) openhandedness, generosity, and hospitality; (3) self-indulgence; (4) sentimentality, and even romanticism; (5) gregariousness; (6) materialism; (7) confidence and self-confidence; (8) complacency, bordering occasionally on arrogance; (9) cultivation of the competitive spirit; (10) indifference to, and exasperation with laws, rules, and regulations; (11) equalitarianism; and (12) resourcefulness (pp. 246-254).

What about Canadian character as opposed to what Commager stated above? To help us in this regard, a generation ago, Lipset (1973) made a perceptive comparison between the two countries. After stating that they probably resemble each other more than any other two countries in the world, he asserted that there seemed to be a rather "consistent pattern of differences between them" (p. 4). He found that certain "special differences" did exist and may be singled out as follows:

> Varying origins in their political systems and national identities, varying religious traditions, and varying frontier experiences. In general terms, the value orientations of Canada stem from a counterrevolutionary past, a need to differentiate itself from the United States, the influence of Monarchical institutions, a dominant Anglican religious tradition, and a less individualistic and more governmentally controlled expansion of the Canadian than of the American frontier (p. 5).

What Happened to the Original Enlightenment Ideal?

The achievement of "the good life" for a majority of citizens in the developed nations, a good life that involves a creative and constructive use of leisure as a key part of general education, necessarily implies that a certain type of progress has been made in society. However, we should understand that the chief criterion of progress has undergone a subtle but decisive change since the founding of the United States republic, for example. This development has had a definite influence on Canada and Mexico as well. Such change has been at once a cause and a reflection of the current disenchantment of some with technology. Recall that the late 18th century was a time of political revolution when monarchies, aristocracies, and the ecclesiastical structure were being challenged on a number of fronts in the Western world. Also, the factory system was undergoing significant change at that time. Such industrial development with its greatly improved machinery "coincided with the formulation and diffusion of the modern Enlightenment idea of history as a record of progress. . . ." (Marx, 1990, p. 5).

Thus, this "new scientific knowledge and accompanying technological power was expected to make possible a comprehensive improvement in all of the conditions of life--social, political, moral, and intellectual as well as material." This idea did indeed slowly take hold and eventually "became the fulcrum of the dominant American world view" (Marx, p. 5). By 1850, however, with the rapid growth of the United States especially, the idea of progress was already being dissociated from the Enlightenment vision of political and social liberation.

Technology and Life Improvement.

By the turn of the twentieth century, "the technocratic idea of progress [had become] a belief in the sufficiency of scientific and technological innovation as the basis for general progress" (Marx, p. 9). This came to mean that if scientific-based technologies were permitted to develop in an unconstrained manner, there would be an automatic improvement in all other aspects of life! What happened--because this theory became coupled with onrushing, unbridled capitalism--was that the ideal envisioned by Thomas Jefferson in the United States had been turned upside down. Instead of social progress being guided by such values as justice, freedom, and self-fulfillment for all people, rich or poor, these goals of vital interest in a democracy were subjugated to a burgeoning society dominated by supposedly more important *instrumental* values (i.e., useful or practical ones for advancing a capitalistic system).

So the fundamental question still today is, "which type of values will win out in the long run?" In North America, for example, it seems that a gradually prevailing concept of cultural relativism was increasingly discredited as the 1990s witnessed a sharp clash between (1) those who uphold so-called Western cultural values and (2) those who by their presence are dividing the West along a multitude of ethnic and racial lines. This is occasioning strong efforts to promote fundamentalistic religions and sects--either those present historically or those recently imported--characterized typically by decisive right/wrong morality.

Postmodernism as an Influence

The orientation and review of selected world, European, North American, regional, and local developments occurring in the final quarter of the 20th century might seem a bit out of place to some who read this book. It could be asked whether this has a relationship to the value system in place in North America. My response to this question is a resounding "Yes." The affirmative answer is correct, also. if we listen to the voices of those in the minority within philosophy who are seeking to practice their profession, or promote their discipline. as if it had some connection to the world as it exists. I am referring here, for example to a philosopher like Richard Rorty (1997). He, as a so-called Neo-pragmatist, exhorts the presently "doomed Left" in North America to join the fray again. Their presumed shame should not be bolstered by a mistaken belief that only those who agree with the Marxist position that capitalism must be eradicated are "true Lefts." Rorty seems truly concerned that philosophy once again become characterized as a "search for wisdom," a search that seeks conscientiously and capably to answer the myriad of questions looming before humankind all over the world.

While most philosophers have been "elsewhere engaged," what has been called postmodernism has become a substantive factor in intellectual circles. I must confess up front that I've been grumbling about--and seeking to grapple with--the term "postmodern" for years. Somehow it has now become as bad (i.e., misunderstood or garbled) as existentialism, pragmatism, idealism, etc.). I confess, also, that I have now acquired a small library on the topic. At any rate, I recently read *Crossing the Postmodern Divide* by Albert Borgman (Chicago, 1992). I was so pleased to find something like this assessment of the situation. I say this because, time and again, I have encountered what I would characterize as gobbledygook describing what has been called "civilization's plight." By that I mean that what I encountered time and again was technical jargon, almost seemingly deliberate obfuscation by people seemingly trying to "fool the public" on this topic. As I see it, if it's worth saying, it must be said carefully and understandably. Otherwise one can't help but think that the writer is a somewhat confused person.

At any rate, in my opinion this effort by Borgman is solid, down-to-earth, and comprehensible up to the final two pages. At the point he veers to Roman Catholicism as the answer to the plight of moderns. It is his right, of course, to state his personal opinion after describing the current situation so accurately. However, if he could have brought himself to it, or if he had thought it might be possible, I would have preferred it if he had spelled out several alternative, yet still other desirable directions for humankind to consider in the 21st century.

Is this modern epoch or era coming to an end? An epoch approaches closure when many of the fundamental convictions of its advocates are challenged by a substantive minority of the populace. It can be argued that indeed the world is moving into a new epoch as the proponents of postmodernism have been affirming over recent decades. Within such a milieu there are strong indications that all professions are going to have great difficulty crossing this so-called, postmodern gap (chasm, divide, whatever!). Scholars argue that many in democracies, under girded by the various rights being propounded (e.g., individual freedom, privacy), have come to believe that they require a supportive "liberal consensus" within their respective societies.

Post-modernists now form a substantive minority that supports a more humanistic, pragmatic, liberal consensus in society. Within such a milieu there are strong indications that present-day society is going to have difficulty crossing the "designated," postmodern divide. Traditionalists in democratically oriented political systems may not like everything they see in front of them today, but as they look elsewhere they flinch even more. After reviewing where society has been, and where it is now, two more questions need to be answered. Where is society heading? And. most importantly, where should it be heading?

Some argue that Nietzsche's philosophy of being, knowledge, and morality supports the basic dichotomy espoused by the philosophy of being in the post-modernistic position. I can understand at once, therefore, why it meets with opposition by those whose thought has been supported by traditional theocentrism (i.e., in the final analysis, it is God "who calls the shots."). It can be argued, also, that many in democracies undergirded by the various rights being propounded (e.g., individual freedom, privacy) have come to believe--as stated above--that they require a supportive "liberal consensus." However, conservative, essentialist elements functioning in such political systems feel that the deeper foundation justifying this claim of a requisite, liberal consensus has been never been fully rationalized--keeping their more authoritative orientations in mind, of course. The foundation supporting the more humanistic, pragmatic, liberal consensus, as I understand it, is what may be called postmodernism by some.

Postmodernists subscribe largely to a humanistic, anthropocentric belief as opposed to the traditional theocentric position. They would subscribe, therefore, I think, to what Berelson and Steiner in the mid-1960s postulated as a behavioral science image of man and woman. This view characterized the human as a creature continuously adapting reality to his or her own ends (1964).

Thus, the authority of theological positions, dogmas, ideologies, and some "scientific infallibilism" is severely challenged. A moderate postmodernist--holding a position I feel able to subscribe to once I am able to bring it all into focus--would at least listen to what the "authority" had written or said before criticizing or rejecting it. A strong postmodernist goes his or her own way by early, almost automatic, rejection of tradition. Then this person presumably relies on a personal interpretation and subsequent diagnosis to muster the authority to challenge any or all icons or "lesser gods" extant in society.

If the above is reasonably accurate, it would seem that a postmodernist might well feel more comfortable by seeking to achieve personal goals through a modified or semi-postmodernistic position as opposed to the traditional stifling position of essentialistic theological realists or idealists. A more pragmatic "value-is-that-which-is proven-through-experience" orientation leaves the future open-ended.

Whatever your personal orientation may be, you will be faced with decisions of varying complexity that must be made every day of your life. In Section Two that follows, we will look into this vital matter at some depth. Read on. . . .

SECTION II
The Ethical Decision-Making Dilemma

An intelligent person today understands that most of the world's nations have won a recognizable semblance of victory over what is often a harsh physical environment. Yet many of the world's peoples living within these nations' boundaries have not yet been able to remove much of the insecurity evident in their efforts to live together constructively and peacefully. Why is this so? The book *"Who Knows What's Right Anymore?* (Zeigler, 2002) offers a detailed approach to the answering of this question. There is so much "fractionating division" in the world today. Frankly, the awesome power exerted by the "inherent" ethical systems of the world's organized religions needs to be fully understood, counteracted, and "reconstructed" before the situation can be improved.

Organized religion has continued for millennia as a social force that almost automatically controls the lives of billions of people of the world to a greater or lesser extent. One might argue that this is a good thing, that humankind truly needs the guidance provided by, for example, the "original-sin group" (i.e., the promulgators and adherents of many of the more conservative elements of the world's 13 great religions, along with the innumerable sects within these enterprises). Indeed the need for this "guidance" may well still be present today, and these religious structures are still in place striving mightily to meet the needs and demands made of them. They have been vital in the past, and they are determined to retain their place in modern times.

A second group is increasing in number daily. This second group could well be called the "scientific-ethics group." Its adherents, many of whom give nominal support to one or another established religion, believe that the great religions have had their day. They believe further that humankind had best devise a more effective and efficient way to decide what is right and good in contrast to what is wrong and evil, respectively. In other words, there is strong evidence all around us that similar harsh conditions still exist today--but that revised or new social institutions are needed to meet present-day crises.

Finally, there is another truly substantive group of humans, many who are nominal members of, and give lip service to, one of the 13 (or more!) religions mentioned above. Yet these people typically live their daily lives as though these major religions don't even exist. When it comes to the making of decisions, they almost invariably "shoot from the lip." This is what I am identifying loosely as the "commonsense group."

Ethical Decision-Making

Ethical decision-making--i.e., deciding what is right and good--can indeed be a most provocative subject. When you get right down to it, the trichotomy of "original sin or scientific ethics or common sense" just described is a capsule analysis of the basic choices that the majority of humankind is facing. On the one hand, there are those who believe that some external power, God or his chosen representative, made this basic decision eons ago about right and wrong (and good and evil) for humankind.

On the other hand, there are those who consider such pronouncements to be largely myth or fairy tale. The latter group argues that it is up to us today to create our own "heaven and/or hell." This is to be done presumably through a steady, evolutionary, scientific search for what is good (i.e., workable) and what is bad (unworkable) or what is right or wrong. A third group, perhaps the majority, don't really spend much time worrying about it all. When an ethical problem arises, they use their common sense to arrive at a solution and then "muddle their way through."

Consequently, as a result of this "original sin," "scientific ethics," or "common sense" plight, people of all ages and backgrounds in most societies still find significant disagreement on the subject of human values, morality, and ethics. Nevertheless, there is also substantial evidence that many men and women are diligently and resolutely seeking a sensitive understanding of themselves and their fellows. Yet, as a result of the most divisive, long-standing, basic intra- and intercultural differences in belief that prevail, there is reason to believe that the future of the world society may well be in great danger as the 21st century progresses.

Indeed, it may well be that our "distorting emotions and destructive passions" created by these and other seemingly unsolvable differences represent the "greatest danger" for the future (Burtt, 1965, p. 311). If such a danger does indeed exist, the development and application of a sound, but not too complex, approach to cross-cultural, ethical decision-making in personal and professional living could be of inestimable assistance to people everywhere. This will not occur, however, unless the present inability to shed many archaic beliefs and ideologies is overcome.

No Universal Ethical Foundation Available

Unfortunately, even though many philosophers have searched persistently throughout history for a normative (i.e., standard) ethical system on which people could and should base their conduct, there is still no single, non-controversial foundation accepted universally on which the entire structure of ethics can be based. This need for an acceptable, workable ethical approach is especially true at a time when developments in the field of communications, for example, have thrust us into a situation where the concept of the world as a "global village" has become a reality--in the developed world at least. Any event that is newsworthy becomes almost immediately available through satellite communication to television stations at all points of the globe. As a result, it is becoming increasingly difficult, if not impossible, to view humanity as only an indistinct amalgam of separate cultures able to proceed on their own.

Despite the above, we have witnessed a steadily rising tide of often unreasonably chauvinistic nationalism in recent years throughout the world. This development has been occasioned by an evident need for people to retain strong cultural identities through independent national status. However, because of an accompanying tide of rising expectations, we find many people within these nations--many with dubious political status--becoming part of disenfranchised populations where strife and revolt often prevail. As a result a certain percentage of these men, women, and children are seeking to move where they believe they and their offspring will have a better opportunity for "the good life.'

This turmoil in both developed and/or underdeveloped nations has created serious problems for the world, at large. Of course, this holds true, also, for the United States, Canada, and Mexico here in our North American culture. On this side of the Atlantic, we were supposedly entering an age of leisure in the industrialized world in the 1960s, but today there's a completely different outlook confronting us as we struggle in the throes of emergence as postindustrial nations. Resultantly, this continent is rapidly becoming a vast multiethnic culture peopled by individuals who as they came here brought other-world religious and ethical backgrounds. It would be too visionary, of course, to expect that cultural differentiation would cease tomorrow, and that overnight all would become enthusiastic Americans or Canadians, or Mexicans, respectively. However, it should be possible to work in that direction specifically in a much better manner than we find today.

Also, it does bring home the need to promote steadily improving international relations. Whether the "global village" concept working in certain aspects of society (e.g., economics) will lead to the eventual establishment of one "recognizable" world culture is anybody's guess. However, cross-cultural understanding must be cultivated with great diligence. I believe this is vital because our "global village" now has a blanketing communications network that is steadily and inevitably receiving a perspective of human values and ethics dominated by the outlook of these news-disseminating organizations. This could well be the only hope for human civilization on Earth if people are to live together peacefully in the future. *However, the "message" that goes forth must be beneficent in the final analysis.*

Further, as if the need for such "harmonization" among and between cultures will not be difficult enough in itself, we are at present also witnessing the origins of a new science called evolutionary psychology. This developing field, based on the investigations of evolutionary biologists and a variety of social-science scholars, presents a strong possibility (probability?) that the end result will be a sharply revised view of human nature itself. Assessing contemporary social reality, Wright (1994) argues that a new understanding of the imperatives required by human genes is needed. Resultantly, it could be that the very foundation of our human concept of goodness will never be the same again.

With thoughts such as these as a backdrop, I have personally "survived" as a presumably ethical, dual citizen of the United States and Canada, a person who has worked professionally for a total of 60+ years in both countries (first one, then the other, etc.). Yet I have also long since come to the conclusion that we all face a confusing "Tower of Babel" daily. When we are confronted with everyday decision-making about problems of an ethical nature, "confusion prevails." I say this because in our relationships with others we so often seem to be speaking "different languages" about what's right and what's wrong, as well as which actions are good and which are bad.

I have found this statement to be true for many reasons: (1) whether a parent is speaking to a son or daughter about a social-relationship problem in school, (2) whether that same parent is facing a marital problem in the home, (3) whether a member of that family confronts someone with an issue on a neighborhood street, (4) whether the same man or woman has an ethical decision to make at work as a professional practitioner or tradesperson, or (5) whether a person discovers an issue to resolve that has ecological implications. Let's face it, these examples cited just scratch the surface of the many issues and concerns about which the individual is required to make rapid decisions daily.

A Down-to-Earth Approach to Ethics

Seeking to improve what basically amounts to a "cultural impasse," I am offering you here in Section III what I believe to be a down-to-earth approach to help you solve the many personal, social/environmental, and professional problems face us all from one day to the next. I must confess immediately that I have wandered far afield from the stated or implied "religious ethics" of my upbringing as a Protestant (Lutheran, Baptist, and agnostic Unitarian-Universalist in that order). Over time I have found present in me a strong, steadily growing belief that we (all people in the developing world) must somehow-- and relatively soon--rise above this or that sectarian religious or ideological position. As the world is turning, indeed we must--if we ever hope to have a peaceful world--seek a workable level of normative consensus among the often conflicting ethical beliefs of the world's leading religions and ideologies.

Trained philosophers, especially those of the "analytic persuasion" may well view this practical approach as reductionistic (i.e., abridged and overly simplified). Such an assessment would only be true to a degree, since the first phase of this approach to ethical decision-making should not be new or completely antithetical to them. In fact, it is a well-considered plan that was used for many years with college undergraduates (**by Prof. Richard Fox of Cleveland State University**). He did so because he felt that an elementary, straightforward plan at least got reasonably intelligent students off to a good start with the subject of applied ethics. *Of course, how they subsequently approached ethical decision-making as they matured could well be another matter.*

So, if you will grant what I stated originally above as an apparent truth--i.e., the moral confusion that prevails currently in North America and elsewhere in much of the world--I will assume further that all who read these words will be interested also in improving society's educational process in this aspect of general education. Basically, I am arguing that all children and young people in our society should have the opportunity to develop their own rational powers through the finest possible, competency-based educational experience relating to ethics and morality. (I might add that I am not for a minute recommending any retroactive change in the separation of church and state where it already exists, but I do believe that some basic agreement regarding the subject-matter of ethics, as well as about an appropriate, accompanying teaching methodology, is needed urgently so that this subject may be taught within public education at all levels.)

Any new approach being recommended needs solid justification. I believe strongly that such a case can be made for the approach recommended here for North America--as a point of departure. In the first place, I have tried it out personally and professionally over a period of years in class with my own university students, and it worked very well basically. Experience indicated where certain modifications were advisable, and these changes were made and have also been incorporated here.

I do recommend here initially one approach (a three-step one) of a normative nature for experimentation since it is quite consistent with the historical values and norms of North American society to this point. However I should make it crystal-clear, also, that even though I will shortly point you toward consideration of a scientific-ethics approach, each person should, in the final analysis, work this out for himself or herself. (This seems only fair, since sensitive understanding in essential to treat a subject that is undoubtedly highly controversial and taught "at one's peril" presently in public education.)

In the experiential educational process recommended here, the hope is that reason will begin to act as the programmer of the young person's "emotional computer" as soon as possible in his or her life. Our primary concern as parents or teachers should, of course, be to help the boy or girl to develop conscious convictions in which the mind leads and the emotions follow. In this way the maturing person would gradually learn what values are important to him or to her. As Ayn Rand (1960) explained, "the integrated sum of a person's basic values is that person's sense of life" (p. 35).

To cite one important example where improved ethical decision-making is needed, permit me to describe a subject that I know very well, competitive sport. It has become increasingly apparent to me that there is an urgent need for those involved in highly competitive sport to understand and then to develop a greatly improved approach to sport ethics and morality. Social institutions (e.g., religion, economics, education) are presumed to be beneficial to society as a whole--not detrimental! Yet as I see it, if we expect beneficial transfer of training to occur, highly competitive sport as a social institution may currently be doing more harm than good in the promotion of sound human relations and development. (This assertion is made about commercialized sport in public education and professional sport in the United States especially, but it undoubted applies to professional sport everywhere).

Thus, because of what I have assessed as a steadily deteriorating situation in U.S. competitive sport, I strongly believe that the development of a proper understanding of the prevailing "immoral" situation in U.S. is very important for athletes, coaches, athletic administrators, game officials, teachers, students, educational administrators, governing board members, local citizens, state or provincial legislators, and all the citizens of the nation. As I see it, also, a farsighted plan should be developed first from the standpoint of the possible contribution of ethical instruction to the general education of young people who may strive to be athletes in society. Also, such a plan should be developed so that this subject can be introduced as a requirement in those professional preparation programs in which coaches and physical educators are trained.

The Young Person's "Sense of Life"

Returning to the developing young person and a general education perspective, consider this analysis of what occurs before any semblance of a rational philosophy develops. In this analogy, offered by Ayn Rand, she delineates first the youthful human's possession of a "psychological recorder," that which is truly the person's inherent subconscious, integrating mechanism. This so-called "sense of life" she views as "a pre-conceptual equivalent of metaphysics, an emotional, subconsciously integrated appraisal of man and existence." As she sees it, this determines "the nature of a man's emotional responses and the essence of his character" (p. 31).

What the young person really needs at this juncture of his or her development is an "intellectual roadbed" that provides a "course of life" to follow. The eventual goal should be a fully integrated personality, a person whose mind and emotions are in harmony a great deal of the time. When this occurs, we find a situation where the individual's sense of life matches his or her conscious convictions. It is fundamental further, of course, that the young person's view of reality be carefully defined by himself or herself and is reasonably consistent. And, the argument continues, if ethical instruction was planned more carefully and explicitly, the quality of living would probably be greatly improved for all.

As I believe is happening today in North America, we have been led, most unfortunately, to the point where the child or young person typically learns to make rational ethical decisions poorly and inadequately. I strongly believe that this is a tragic condition because the young person's all-important personality development is so often misdirected, misguided, and at least temporarily stunted.

Summary

In summary, I have argued here that we require a steadily improving crop of young citizens and professional people whose general education and professional education is under girded by sound theory based on solid research and scholarly endeavor. Moreover, and perhaps more important ultimately, I have argued further that all of this will be in vain if we do not turn out high-calibre young people with high ethical standards. Thus we are faced with the urgent need to make certain that such ethical sensitivity will be attained as a required competency by those who emerge from our educational system.

So there it is. Recognizing and appreciating that values, ethics, and morality are a vital part of our heritage, present living, and our future, I hope that you will be helped by this volume to forge an improved personal and professional approach to ethical decision-making in your life. If you do, the end result should be a more satisfying and rewarding existence for you. It should also have implications for your family, as well as for your friends and business associates. In Section Three that follows, after explaining that ethical decision-making can be subdivided into three categories (personal, professional, and environmental), I will describe briefly the six major approaches to ethical decision-making extant in North America.

SECTION III
From Personal to Professional to Environmental Ethics

Rapid Change Brings Ethical Confusion

The main purpose of this section is twofold. First, I want to point out that there are basically three types of ethical decisions that we are called upon to make. I have designated these decisions as (1) personal, (2) professional, and (3) environmental Second, I will offer you a bird's-eye view of six of the major routes to ethical decision-making that are available in the Western world today.

As explained previously, rapid change in society had caused general confusion about the subject of ethics. As Miller (n.d.) pointed out in his "The Tangle of Ethics," "Instead of having an impossible ideal confronting a practical necessity, we have such a diverse inheritance of ethical ways that no matter which one we choose, the others are at least to some degree betrayed." Obviously, this confusion has been exacerbated because of the complex of moral systems that we have inherited (e.g., Hebraic, Christian, Renaissance, Industrial--and now Islam too, for example).

This confusion has been gradually, but steadily, carried over into all aspects of life. Further, as we now comprehend that the 20th century was indeed one of marked transition from one era to another, some scholars are beginning to understand that America's quite blind philosophy of optimism about history's malleability and compatibility in keeping with North American ideals may turn out to be very shortsighted. At least the weapons stalemate between the U.S.A. and the former U.S.S.R. brought to prominence the importance of nonmilitary determinants (e.g., politics and ideologies). Most important, also, the world is conversely witnessing the gradual, but seemingly inevitable, development of a vast ecological crisis, a dilemma that is increasingly causing a number of health and financial problems to the highly industrialized nations especially.

It may well be impossible to gain objectivity and true historical perspective on the rapid change that is taking place. Nevertheless, a seemingly unprecedented burden of increasing complexity has been imposed on people's understanding of themselves and their world. Many leaders, along with the rest of us, must certainly be wondering whether the whole affair can be managed. I repeat here (for emphasis) the earthshaking developments of the decades immediately preceding the 1990s. Naisbitt (1982) outlined the "ten new directions that are transforming our lives," as well as the "megatrends" insofar as women's evolving role in societal structure (Aburdene & Naisbitt, 1992):

(1) the concepts of the information society and the Internet,
(2) "high tech/high touch,"
(3) the shift to world economy,
(4) the need to shift to long-term thinking in regard to ecology,
(5) the move toward organizational decentralization,
(6) the trend toward self-help,
(7) the ongoing discussion of the wisdom of participatory democracy as opposed to representative democracy,
(8) a shift toward networking,
(9) a reconsideration of the "north-south" orientation, and
(10) the viewing of decisions as "multiple option" instead of "either/or."

Add to this the increasing, lifelong involvement of women in the workplace, politics, sports, organized religion, and social activism, and we begin to understand that a new world order has descended upon us for the 21st century.

Moving ahead in time slightly, here again is a second list of 10 issues facing political leaders was highlighted in the *Utne Reader* titled "Ten events that shook the world between 1984 and 1994" (1994). pp. 58-74). Just consider the following:

(1) the fall of communism (USSR) and the continuing rise of nationalism,
(2) the environmental crisis and the green movement,
(3) the AIDS epidemic and the "gay response,"
(4) continuing wars (29 in 1993) and the peace movement,

(5) the gender war,
(6) religion and racial tension,
(7) the concept of "West meets East" and resultant implications,
(8) the "Baby Boomers" came of age and "Generation X" has started to worry and complain because of declining expectation levels,
(9) the whole idea of globalism and international markets, and
(10) the computer revolution and the specter of Internet.

Keeping these changes and developments in mind, in the realm of economics the world's "manageability" may have nevertheless been helped by its division into three major trading blocs: (1) the Pacific Rim dominated by Japan, (2) the European Community very heavily influenced by Germany, and (3) North America dominated by the United States of America.

Impending Cultural Clashes

While economics may be helping the world's "manageability," some observers argue interestingly that perhaps something even more fundamental has occurred. Succinctly put, world politics seems to be "entering a new phase in which the fundamental source of conflict will be neither ideological nor economic." So stated Samuel P. Huntington (1993), of Harvard's Institute for Strategic Studies, who believes that now the major conflicts in the world will actually be clashes between different groups of civilizations espousing fundamentally different cultures.

These clashes, Huntington states, represent a distinct shift away from viewing the world as being composed of first, second, and third worlds as was the case during the Cold War that began after World War II. Thus, Huntington is arguing that in the 21st century the world will return to a pattern of development evident several hundred years ago in which civilizations will actually rise and fall. (Of course, this movement of civilizations is exactly what was postulated by the late Arnold Toynbee in his famous theory of history.) One thing is certain, however, the world's complexity will increase even more in the 21st century.

Values of a Liberal Society

Keeping growing intercultural complexity in mind, it becomes more important than ever that the values and norms of a liberal society be fully understood by an increasing percentage of the world's population. Such understanding has an obvious direct relationship to the present discussion of personal and professional ethics. I wish I could state, for example, that the field of professional education was ready to meet the challenge of the 21st century. Close to a generation ago, Chazan (1973) stated. "Civil, political, and educational leaders frequently cite education's crucial role in the transmission of those 'moral and spiritual values' necessary for life in today's complex world; yet few educational systems make formal provision for such value education . . ." (p. 1). If education is to serve society more effectively in the 21st century, it is absolutely vital that it become attuned to the greatest possible extent with the values and norms of evolving society in North America.

Values represent the highest echelon of the social system level of the entire social action system. These values may be categorized into such entities as artistic values, educational values, social values, sport values, etc. Of course, in the final analysis, all types or categories of values must be values of, or values held by, personalities. Such social values within our social system are an integral part of a hierarchy of control and conditioning that exerts pressure downward along with the established norms of the social structure (Johnson, 1994). Together they work to maintain the pattern consistency of the entire system while at the same time preserving a reasonable degree of flexibility (pp. 57-58).

The values of the United States' social system are those that are conceived as representative of the ideal general character that is desired by those who ultimately hold the power in this society (Bayles, 1981). Arguing from the premise that citizens are reasonable people, we can accept that "the chief values relevant to professional ethics are (1) governance by law, (2) freedom, (3) protection from injury, (4) equality of opportunity, (5) privacy, and (6) welfare" (p. 5).

Norms, in this context a term not well understood generally, are developed in societies as a result of the values that are consensually held. In sociological perspective, they are the shared, sanctioned rules that govern the second level of the social structure. (Incidentally, the laws of a country are typically based on the norms held.) The average person finds it difficult to separate the concept of values from that of norms (Johnson, 1969). Some examples of norms in the United States are (1) the institution of private property, (2) private enterprise, (3) the monogamous conjugal family, and (4) the separation of church and state (pp. 46-58).

The Professions: Yesterday and Today

To place the topic of professions in brief historical perspective, recall that the idea of professions and rudimentary preparation for such occupations in life (e.g., military, religious) originated in the very early societies . Early centers for a type of professional instruction were developed in ancient Greece and Rome as elementary bodies of knowledge became available. It wasn't until approximately the midpoint of the Middle Ages, however, that universities were organized where the various embryonic professional groups banded together for convenience, power, and protection (Brubacher, 1962). The degree granted at that time was in itself a license to practice whatever it was that the graduate "professed"--a practice that continued during the Renaissance at which time the instruction offered became increasingly secularized. However, the term "profession" was not commonly used until relatively recently (p. 47 et ff.).

Such background provides a perspective; but what is a profession today? Many different meanings are offered, but a profession is usually described as a vocation (a word derived from Latin meaning a "calling") that requires specific mastery of knowledge of some aspect of learning before the prospective practitioner is accepted as a professional person. The now legendary Abraham Flexner (1915) recommended six criteria as being characteristic of a profession, but Bayles (1981)--on whose work I lean heavily immediately below--maintained that there is still no definition of the term that is generally accepted at present. Keeping in that there are categories of recognized professions such as consulting, scholarly, performing, etc., he suggested an approach whereby necessary features are indicated along with a number of other common features that would tend to elevate an occupation to professional status.

A profession includes typically those people who are functioning in a subdisciplinary and/or subprofessional category within it (e.g., medicine, law, psychology). Merely stating that a group of people working within a field of endeavor at the public, semipublic or private levels represent a profession is only a beginning, of course. There is obviously much more to be accomplished than that (Bayles, 1981). It can be argued, however, that there is no generally acceptable definition for a profession today--i.e., it is evidently impossible to characterize professions by a set of necessary and sufficient features possessed by all professions--and only by professions (Bayles, 1981, p. 7). Nevertheless, the following is a brief attempt to define what constituted a profession in the last quarter of the 20th century:

> (1) A profession can be defined as an occupation which requires specific knowledge of some aspect of learning before a person is accepted as a professional person.
>
> (2) There are categories of professions as follows: consulting, teaching, research, performing, etc.
>
> (3) The following may be considered as three necessary features of an occupation that can also be designated as a profession: (i) a need for extensive training; (ii) a significant intellectual component that must be mastered; and (iii) a recognition by society that the trained person can provide an important basic service.

Additionally, there are some other features that are common to most professions as follows: (4) licensing by state/province or professional body, (5) establishment of professional societies, (6) considerable autonomy in work performance, and (7) establishment of a creed or code of ethics.

> (**Note**: A most important component of a comprehensive code of ethics is that the controlling body establish an ethics committee to which infractions of the ethical code may be reported for deliberation and possible disciplinary action.)

Also, most professions typically have a good deal of autonomy in their work, but those who work in large organizations often feel constrained in their efforts by too much red tape. Finally, there are additional salient features that characterize professions (e.g., near monopoly of services, research, and publication).

A very few professions are better than all others in regard to the availability of codes of ethics. By this I mean that they not only have codes of ethics spelled out carefully already, but they have also instituted ways and means of disciplining errant members who violate one or more provisions of their respective codes. Fortunately, in those professions where practitioners have an ever-present opportunity to "do harm" as well as to "do good" to their clients, society has instituted laws to protect people from malpractice (e.g., medicine, law).

We need to keep in mind further that some professions are immediately recognized as such (e.g., law);

some groups are striving for such status (e.g., management); and some groups tend to call themselves professionals when uncertainty still prevails in the mind of the public. In the course of their development, the various, often embryonic, professional groups have gradually become conscious of the need for a code of ethics. By this is meant a set of professional obligations (i.e., duties) that are established as norms for practitioners in good standing to follow. The code of ethics itself is based on standards of virtue and vice (e.g., honesty, truthfulness) from which quite general principles of responsibility are outlined as a basis for specific rules of duty are detailed carefully.

Codes have usually conformed to one of two types or patterns that have been handed down over the centuries. As Hazard (1978) explained,

> One pattern is that of a creed or affirmation of professional belief. The ethical principles of medicine or social work, for example, are stated this way. The creed is short and obscure, but lofty, expressing the aims of the profession and adjuring personal commitment to them--a kind of oath of vocational office. The other pattern is the legal code. Not surprisingly, this is the ethical format in the legal profession; to an increasing extent it is being adopted in accountancy. It may be described as a set of detailed administrative regulations. . . .(pp. 50-51).

Hazard explained further that in some cases the regulations are spelled out by the profession itself, whereas in others it is a governmental or public policy that take the lead. Further, the creed seems to have been accepted as a better approach than the code because of its generality, and since it doesn't confine the professional person unduly. However, he believed definitely that neither the creed nor the code has spoken too "intelligibly to the fundamental ethical problems arising in the professions" [or in a trade for that matter] (pp. 50-51).

A Plan for the Future

We may be willing to grant that there is indeed a "tangle of ethics" as stated by Miller above. We can grant, also, that the field of education has been wary about the introduction of ethical and moral values in the school curriculum because of the separation of church and state tradition that has prevailed on this continent. Nevertheless, there is no sound reason for professional educators not to introduce a required course in professional ethics for every person preparing for one of the professions. By this point you, the reader, may well agree with the stance recommended here. A knowledge of right and wrong ethical behavior would appear to be vital for every prospective practitioner in a profession.

For those people already out in the field, interesting and informative programs about ethical behavior should be arranged at annual professional meetings--programs where matters of serious ethical concern and import are placed up front for in-depth consideration, deliberation, and decision. Regional and state (or provincial) clinics on ethical topics are another means whereby we can make up for lost time, for our possible sins of omission in this regard. Still further, we should make an effort to have discussions on ethical matters of all types included in any certification programs that are being made available for practitioners.

When I, as a former university professor, first became involved with the question of professional ethics 30 years ago, I turned to the American Association of University Professors to which I belonged before moving back to Canada. I uncovered the "Statement on Professional Ethics" that had been endorsed by the membership at the 52nd Annual Meeting of the AAUP (1969). It was very brief and was in essence a creed rather than a code (as explained above).

As I learned, this "Statement" was "necessarily presented in terms of the ideal" and referred (1) to the responsibilities placed upon the professor as the advancement of knowledge is pursued; (2) to the need to encourage "the free pursuit of learning in his (sic) students"; (3) to the "obligations that derive from common membership in the community of scholars"; (4) to the obligation to seek "above all to be an effective teacher and scholar"; and (5) to the fact that he has "the rights and obligations of any citizen" (pp. 86-87). This is a fine statement of a creed (i.e., a brief statement of belief). Nevertheless, I ask to what extent it ever referred to by anyone. Also, I felt the lack of guidance offered because of the omission of any standards, principles, or rules that should flow from the statement of a professor's obligations.

Next I turned for possible assistance from statements that made available periodically by a selected number of professions. These statements varied in length and were often more specific that the creed offered by the AAUP. For example, in the law profession, the American Bar Association's Model Rules of Personal Conduct are lengthy and highly detailed. Conversely, the American Medical Association's Principles of Medical Ethics are envisioned briefly as seven principles or standards of conduct underlying honorable behavior. The American Nurses' Association Code for Nurses is very similar to that of the AMA in regard to length and the approach taken.

The American Society for Public Administrators approaches this subject somewhat differently again, however. It offered a *Workbook and Study Guide for Public Administrators* that concluded with a discussion about the background, definitions, and recommended key principles of professional ethics. Finally, to confirm my belief that no standardization had occurred among the many professions, I examined the American Psychological Association's Ethical Principles of Psychologists and the National Society of Professional Engineers' Code of Ethics for Engineers. The former (APA) included a relatively brief preamble followed by a statement of 10 carefully defined principles, whereas the latter (NSPE) was somewhat more detailed and included preamble, fundamental canons or virtues, rules of practice, and professional obligations.

Despite the evident need for creeds and codes of ethics for the almost innumerable list of professions, trades, occupations, jobs, or whatever, my conclusion, based on discussions with colleagues in my field and in others, was that there is great room for progress or improvement. Practically no one with whom I talked knew anything about the subject as it applied to his or her own profession or occupation. Also, I discovered that, although many professional societies had at some point gone through the motions of establishing creeds and (shorter or longer) codes of ethics, only a very small percentage of these professional groups has established standing disciplinary committees to deal with possible infractions of their codes of ethics (e.g., medicine, law, and psychology). In other words, we have "nowhere to go but up!"

Today we often hear about the need for a pursuit of excellence in North America, about how we aren't living up to standards that have been set. To me this means that we do indeed want to develop outstanding students in our many education programs. Yet I also have serious concerns about the type of knowledge, competencies, and related skills that we expect students to master. Further, this statement applies strongly also to the professional education of students. We want all students to be motivated by a desire for excellence, to the limit of their potential.

However, and most importantly, over and above such "excellence," however defined, we must have students who employ a sound ethical approach personally and environmentally. These young people should then go on to their lifelong careers with the necessary knowledge and attitudes that will result in their having a sound base in professional ethics as well. Failing this, any outstanding professional person--at any given moment--could deliberately or unwittingly by dishonesty, immorality, incompetence, or lack of correct action negate any technical excellence gained in a classroom, laboratory environment, or on-the-job experience.

What Are The Major Ethical Routes Available Today?

Before we take a look at the major ethical routes available in the Western world today, there should be no difficulty in reaching agreement on three points. First, a person in our society should be so educated that he or she can reason well--i.e. should have an opportunity to develop rationality as a "life competency." Second, it is most important for a young person to bridge the gap between immaturity and maturity insofar as ethical understanding is concerned. Third, we would expect further that the opportunity to achieve such comprehension within reasonable limits would be readily available to all aspiring young people in North American life today.

Unfortunately, I am forced to state that, despite the fact that you, the reader, may have nodded in agreement theoretically to the three points immediately above, actually achieving such agreement in practice as to (1) what type of competency and (2) how such competency is attained is a completely different matter. I say this because, based on my experience teaching young people for more than half a century, I am forced to concur with the late Ayn Rand's (1960) assertion that on all sides we find young people "integrating blindly, incongruously, and at random" (p. 33) about all aspects of life.

No matter whether the question is (1) taking (or not taking) drugs for presumably heightened experiences, (2) cheating (or not cheating) on examinations or term papers, or (3) breaking (or not breaking) the letter or the spirit of the rules in (e.g., in competitive sport) in one or more than a dozen overt or covert ways, the evidence points to an upbringing in which the very large majority of young persons has not received a type of educational experience in which an acceptable level of "ethical competency" could be developed or has been the result.

I am arguing that it would be extremely difficult to obtain such competency at present. First, a chronological analysis of several sources indicates initially that there is great variation in terminology and emphases. Terms that appear include (1) ethical naturalism, ethical non-naturalism (or intuitionism), and emotivism (Hospers, 1953, p. 485); (2) a recommendation from Patterson (1957) that we can delineate correctly two division or categories of ethical theories (i.e., where the knowledge comes from, and the motive that prompts action); (3) adjectives offered by Fletcher (1966, pp. 17-18) such as legalistic, antinomian, and situational; and (4) those offered by Fromm (1967, p. 37) called authoritarianism, relativism, and scientific ethics.

Moving ahead chronologically with (5) in this welter of terms and descriptive adjectives used to describe ethical stances, Titus and Keaton (1973, pp. 59-60) used a threefold classification, but in the process did their best to avoid an "ism" nomenclature by suggesting that there are those who lives under the aegis of codes (e.g., God's word); those who thrust codes aside and prescribe laws; and those who seek to establish ethical norms through the application of reflective moral judgment. Despite this plea to avoid "isms," Abelson and Friquegnon (1975) recommended ("a no. 6" in this progression) use of such terms as religious absolutism, conventionalism, rational absolutism, and utilitarian relativism. That there is a good deal of commonality in the thought of these ethicists despite different terminology becomes apparent as they are analyzed further. (Obviously, understanding and/or mastering these terms is almost an impossibility for a person outside of the discipline of philosophy.)

To add to this review of what might be called secondary listings arising from the period between 1950 and 1975, I examined pertinent work of a primary nature as follows: John Dewey (1929, 1932, 1946, and 1948); G.E. Moore (1948); Simone de Beauvoir (1964); A.J. Ayer (1946); C.L. Stevenson (1947-48), Joseph Fletcher (1966); J.O. Urmson, (1968); Kurt Baier (1970); and John Rawls (1971).

Then I moved to what might be called the "next generation" of ethicists, those who were publishing from 1970 to 1990. Some of these philosophers whose work I checked were: J. Gouinlock (1972); D. McLellan (1977); T.C. Anderson (1979); W. Hardie (1980); J. Mackie (1980); J. Annas (1981); S. Starker (1981); R. Hayman (1982); R. Hibler (1982); P. Redpath (1983); M. Baron (1984); F. Berger, (1984); D. Farrell (1985); R. Martin (1985); P. Gardner (1988); and R.M. Fox & J.P. DeMarco (1990).

Finally, to assure that the above ethicists identified were standing the test of time, I reviewed the primary works included in the seventh edition of *Great traditions in ethics* by Denise and Peterfreund (1992). As a result of this analysis, six different approaches were selected for inclusion here. Each approach or "ethical route" is described according to:

        (1) underlying presupposition,
        (2) criterion for evaluation,
        (3) method for determination of ethical decision, and
        (4) presumed result.

(Next page, please)

I. AUTHORITARIANISM
(OR LEGALISM)

Underlying Presupposition

> Absolute good and rightness are either present in the world, or have been determined by custom, law, or code.

Criterion for Evaluation

> The criterion is conformity or compliance with rules, laws, moral codes, and established systems and customs in the society or culture involved.

Method for Determination of Ethical Decisions

> Ethical decision-making is carried out by application of the prevailing normative standard or law.

Probable Result

> The solution to any ethical dilemma can be readily determined by strict application of the evaluative criterion.
>
> > (**Note:** Legalism has dominated Christianity [and other orthodox religions] since its early days; thus, it is usually a question of strict obedience to rigid rules and/or laws. For example, homosexuals were burned to death in the Middle Ages, and also condemned to death through some means of torture in Old Testament descriptions. This sort of treatment probably occasioned remarks such as the "immorality of morality" [Henry Miller] and "the moral Majority are the people our ancestors came from Europe to escape" [Gloria Steinem].)

II. RELATIVISM
(OR ANTINOMIANISM)

Underlying Presupposition

>Good or bad, and rightness and wrongness, are relative and vary according to the situation or culture involved.

Criterion for Evaluation

>The needs of a situation there and then in the culture or society concerned are the determining factors as to the values or norms applied to a problematic situation.

Method for Determination of Ethical Decisions

>Guidance in the making of ethical decisions may come from "outside," intuition, one's own conscience, empirical investigation, reasons, etc.

Probable Result

>Each ethical situation will be adjudged in a highly individualistic way, since every situation has its particularity. There are no absolutely valid principles or universal laws.

>(**Note**: It is important not to confuse ethical relativism with cultural relativism. The former denies the presence of any one basic moral principle in the universe, whereas the latter relates to cultural mores [e.g., the South Sea tribe situation where elders are killed at a time when their bodies are still in quite good condition so that they will have a better afterlife].)

III. SITUATIONISM
(AN ECLECTIC "NEW" MORALITY)

Underlying Presupposition

> God's love, or some other summum bonum (i.e., highest good) is an absolute norm. As a result, reason, revelation, and precedent have no objective normative status.

Criterion for Evaluation

> "What is fitting" in any problematic situation is based on the application of agapeic love (Christian love or God's love). There are subordinate moral principles that serve to illuminate the situation further, so that the most accurate evaluation of the problematic situation is made.

Method for Determination of Ethical Decisions

> The resolution of an ethical dilemma results from the use of a calculating method in addition to what might be called contextual appropriateness. The individual should act from loving concern for others (i.e., what is benevolent is right).

Probable Result

> The best solution, everything considered, will result from the application situationally of the principle of God's love (Agape).
>
> **(Note:** Agape can be manifested only when (1) there is awareness of the relevant facts, (2) the likely consequences are calculated, and (3) the guidance of traditional norms is considered.)

IV. SCIENTIFIC ETHICS

Underlying Presupposition

> With the application of scientific method to an ethical situation (to the greatest possible extent), there is no distinction between moral goods and natural goods. The presupposition is that scientific method can bring about complete agreement in due time based on factual belief about what constitutes the most effective and efficient behavior.

Criterion for Evaluation

> Ideas that are helpful in the solution of problematic situations are therefore true. Thus, the empirical verification of a given hypothesis brings a union of theory and practice.

Method for Determination of Ethical Decisions

> The scientific method is applied to problem-solving in ethics. First, reflective thinking results in ideas that then function as tentative solutions for concrete problems. These hypotheses are then tested experimentally to the greatest possible extent, keeping in mind that fallible human beings are involved.

Probable Result

> The assumption is that agreement in factual belief resulting from the application of scientific method will soon bring about agreement in attitude on the part of the majority of the people. n this way we would have continuous adaptation of values based on the culture's changing needs. In time this would effect the directed reconstruction of all social institutions as necessary.
>
> (**Note**: Considering the crisis in human values existing at present, this approach [or some variation thereof] should receive consideration at present. It is evident that earlier confidence in religion and philosophy has been undermined. Also, it is becoming increasingly obvious that science and technology have brought humankind to the point where human life on Earth could be destroyed permanently.)

V. THE "GOOD REASONS" APPROACH

Underlying Presupposition

> Baier's "good reasons" approach, which has also been called the "moral point of view," states that ethical action should be supported by the best reasons (i.e., good reasons, or facts some of which are superior to others). Moral reasons (good reasons) are superior to reasons of immediate pleasure and reasons that are selfish.

Criterion for Evaluation

> All must be subject to the same rules, and rules must be for the good of everyone alike. In the making of an ethical decision, the person involved should (1) not be selfish, (2) make a decision on principle, (3) be willing to universalize this principle; and (4) consider the good of everyone alike. Ethical rules employed in this fashion would quite frequently require people to make sacrifices.

Method for Determination of Ethical Decisions

> This approach to ethical decision-making may be implemented in two stages: (1) by surveying the facts to determine which are relevant, and (2) the weighing of the facts to determine their relative weight in the deliberations to follow. First, the decision-maker is confronted with "consideration-making beliefs" or "rules of reason." These are the major premises of the "inference-licenses" to be considered. The minor premises are other facts which, when matched with the above, help the person to conclude which are the best reason(s). The presence of a specific fact as a consideration accordingly implies the context or outline of a course of action that is being planned by someone.

> Second, the next step involves the weighting of the various "best" reasons that seemed relevant at the first stage. These reasons are "weighed" or evaluated according to what is believed about the superiority of one type of reason over another. Here the hierarchy of reasons is as follows:

> 1. Reasons of self-interest are superior to reasons of momentary pleasure,
> 2. Reasons of long-range interest out balance reasons of short-range interest, and
> 3. Reasons of law, religion, and morality outweigh reasons of self-interest.

Probable Result

> The assumption with this approach is that the individual can reason his or her way through to a

satisfactory method of ethical decision-making. The plan, one that implies first a class of good reasons, moves progressively from (1) reasons of immediate pleasure, to (2) those that are selfish reasons, and, finally, to (3) so-called moral reasons that correlate with the person's long-range interests.

(**Note**: Morality, for Kurt Baier, involves doing things on principle and, as a result, a condition of universal "teachability" could well prevail. Further, the rationale is that moral rules are meant for everyone, and thus they must be for the good of everyone alike. Thus, the "moral point of view" has a relationship to Kant's thought in that the individual should be willing to universalize the principle underlying the action planned.)

(Next page, please)

VI. EMOTIVISM

Underlying Presupposition

> Some have identified emotivism as analytic philosophy's response to the problems of ethics. In this approach, ethics is normative in the sense that there are indeed moral standards. This means, of course, that ethics can never be approached scientifically. The emotivist starts with a real problem, one in which the term "good" appears to be ultimately indefinable. This leads some to claim that use of the word "good" in an ethical sense merely reflects an emotion on the user's part.

Criterion for Evaluation

> An ethical dispute must be on a factual level. It is vital--i.e., absolutely essential--that value statements be distinguished from factual ones.

Method for Determination of Ethical Decision

> Typically, an emotivist approach involves logical analysis (to the extent that this is possible) of ethical (or normative standard) terms, whereas the factual statement in the argument would be based on the most current findings of social science. Next there should be an analysis of conflicting attitudes to determine to what extent progress has been made.

Probable Result

> The assumption is that ethical dilemmas can be resolved reasonably through the combined efforts of the moralist and the social scientist. The hope is that the presence of commonly accepted beliefs will in time bring about change in conflicting attitudes.

>> (**Note:** Undoubtedly this approach has much to offer and merits serious consideration. Its practicality for the average professional person in any field other than philosophy seems questionable. However, one may not have much choice if he or she is having difficulty accepting a specific definition of that elusive term "good.")

Before concluding this section, I decided to arrange the above information about the six different approaches to ethical decision-making in tabular form as well (Table 1 and Table 2 below) so that the reader could make some comparisons as to (1) the underlying suppositions, (2) the criteria used for evaluation, (3) the method used for determination of an ethical decision, and (4) the probable result of any deliberation.

(Next page, please)

Table 1
Comparative Aspects of Major Philosophical Approaches
to Ethical Decision-Making (Part 1)

Decision-Making Approach	Underlying Presupposition	Criterion for Evaluation
I. Authoritarianism (or Legalism)	Absolute good and rightness are either present in the world, or have been determined by custom, law, or code	Conformity to rules, laws, moral codes, established systems. and customs.
II. Relativism (or Antinomianism)	Good and bad, and rightness and wrongness, are relative and vary according to the situation or culture involved.	Needs of situation there and then in culture or society concerned.
III. Situationism (with certain similarity to #1 above)	God's love (or some other summum bonum is an absolute norm; reason, revelation, and precedent have no objective normative status.	"What is fitting" in the situation is based on application of agapeic love; subordinate moral principles serve to illuminate the situation.
IV. Scientific Ethics (scientific method applied to ethics)	No distinction between moral goods and natural goods; science can bring about complete agreement on factual belief about human behavior.	Ideas helpful in solving problematic situations are true; empirical verification of hypothesis should soon bring union of theory and practice.
V. "Good Reasons" (the "moral point of view")	Implies that ethical action should be supported by best reasons (*good*) reasons--i.e., facts superior to others; *moral* reasons superior to other types.	Same rules must be for good of everyone alike; unselfish decisions to be made on principle that can be universalized.
VI. Emotivism (analytic philosophy's	Ethics is normative (i.e., moral standards)	An ethical dispute must be on a factual level;

| response to ethical problems that arise) | and therefore cannot be a science; the term "good" appears to be indefinable. | value statements must be distinguished from factual ones. |

Table 2
Comparative Aspects of Major Philosophical Approaches
to Ethical Decision-Making (Part 2)

Decision-Making Approach	Method for Determination of Ethical Decision	Probable Result
I. Authoritarianism (or Legalism)	Application of normative standard (or law) to resolve the ethical dilemma or issue.	The solution to any ethical dilemma can be readily determined and then implemented (or acted upon).
II. Relativism (or Antinomianism)	Guidance in the making of an ethical decision may come either from "outside"; intuition; one's own conscience; empirical investigation; reason, etc.	Each ethical decision is highly individual since every situation has its particularity; there are no absolutely valid principles
III. Situationism (with certain similarity to #1 above)	Resolution of ethical dilemma results from use of calculating method plus contextual appropriateness; act from loving concern; benevolence = right.	The best solution, everything considered, will result when the principle of God's love is applied situationally
IV. Scientific Ethics (scientific method applied to ethics)	Use of scientific method in problem-solving; reflective thinking begets ideas that function as tentative solutions for for concrete problems; test hypotheses experimentally.	Agreement in factual belief will soon result in agreement in attitude; continuous adaptation of values in the culure's changing needs will result in social change.

V.	"Good Reasons" Approach (the "moral" point of view)	Two stages: (1) determining which facts are relevant; (2) weighing facts to determine relative weight for consideration; a hierarchy of reasons needed.	Assumption is that person can reason way through to a satisfactory method of ethical decision-making using a class of good reasons.
VI.	Emotivism (analytic philosophy's response to ethical problems that arise)	Involves logical analysis of ethical (normative) standard) terms; factual statements referred to social scientists; analyze conflicting attitudes to determine progress.	Ethical dilemma can be resolved through the combined efforts of the moralist and the scientist; common beliefs may in time change attitudes.

Summary

Although all ethical decision-making is a *personal* affair, a distinction was made among ethical decisions that are (1) personal (i.e. between friends and family, etc.), (2) professional (i.e., between colleagues and associates), or (3) in relation to environmental or societal issues and problems.

Then, repeating the argument that it is most important for a developing young person to achieve a level of competency that will enable him or her to employ rationality in arriving at ethical decisions in life, I proceeded to outline--most briefly!--six ethical routes that are available in the Western world at present. I must reiterate that these are not the only approaches available. Nevertheless, a case can be made that they represent a consensual listing (in the West at least).

At this point I believe that I owe the reader an indication of which approach I would personally recommend. There was a time when I made every effort to avoid any such recommendation, because I believed that it was unfair for a teacher to take a strong stand in a society where pluralistic philosophies were permitted and known to prevail. However, the 1960s decade seemed to change all that--for the time being at any rate--as students argued that they "paid their money and had a right to know" where the instructor stood on such-and-such an issue.

In keeping with that (psychological) attitude, a stance that I adopted always with the caveat that I would make every effort to avoid a type of "brainwashing," I freely confess my belief that the application of scientific method to ethical analysis seems necessary at present and on into the foreseeable future. I argue this way because many of us are discovering that there is indeed a "crisis" of human values at this time. The fact is that the confidence that most people had in either religion or philosophy, respectively, has been seriously undermined. Daily we hear on the one hand that science and technology are our great benefactors. Then in the next moment, we learn that science and related technology had shown people ways to actually destroy life on this planet permanently--at least in the sense that we have known human evolution to this point.

Further, we have learned that the 20th century was a transitional one, that the old order has most definitely been replaced by the new! Additionally, what is not generally appreciated is that the rate of change in society appears to be gradually accelerating, and that this acceleration will probably continue to increase. All of this has led me--and innumerable others--to conclude that we must eliminate the persisting *dualism* that exists as soon as possible. What I am referring to, of course, is the dualism that has separated investigation about the physical world from the study of human behavior in relation to moral values and virtues.

Frankly, in this evolving democratic culture within North America, I cannot personally find a strong rationale for any authoritarian or legalistic doctrine governing ethical behavior to prevail (i.e., a doctrine in which ironclad conformity is required because of any individual's or group's presumed knowledge of absolute good and rightness in the world). Such an assumption on my part is a personal one, of course, but I find myself increasingly repelled by the many greater or lesser "ayatollahs" who seek to invade our lives. Here I refer to ministers, priests, rabbis, or (literal) ayatollahs.

It is fortunate for me, I suppose, that our North American society guarantees individual freedom in such matters as long as the laws of the land are not abrogated. (This is not to imply for a moment that the struggle for individual freedom can be given up even momentarily. Actually, not a day goes by even here in

North America that some "enlightened" individual does not request the establishment of some law or regulation for the good of others, typically one that denies individual freedom in one way or another.)

Still further, I have considered the antinomial, relativistic position as well. As pleasant or intriguing as it may be on occasion to rebel against society radically--to the left or right!--antinomianism to me appears to be so far to the left on an authoritarian-anarchistic freedom spectrum as to be fundamentally out of key in the prevailing political and social environment.

Despite the appeal of the emotivist approach (the last of the six described above), including application of the logic of the language analyst, it is my position that society's present plight requires considerably more than just the implementation of this philosophic technique. Conversely, Baier's "good reasons" approach (the so-called "moral point of view") does have appeal and seemingly has something to offer in today's world.

The above notwithstanding--and I fully realize the impossibility of invoking any one approach at this time--I believe strongly that society's failure to employ scientific method in the realm of so-called moral goods, as well as in the obvious realm of so-called natural goods, will keep the North American culture in a position where changes in value will continue to come about either accidentally or arbitrarily.

Structural-functional social theory has alerted us continually about the powerful, controlling influence of societal values and norms. I believe that we should now strive to obliterate the idea that there is a difference in kind between what we have traditionally called "human nature" and what we have identified typically as the "physical world." When such a change in understanding and attitude is accomplished someday (hopefully very soon), we would then really be able to bring the resources of science to bear much more effectively on all human behavior than ever before.

Interestingly, the oft-maligned--but recently rediscovered!--John Dewey explained this 70+ years ago when he asserted that what is needed:

> . . . is intelligent examination of the
> consequences that actually effected by
> inherited institutions and customs, in

> order that there may be intelligent consideration of the ways in which they are to be intentionally modified in behalf of generation of different consequences (1929, pp. 272-273).

Thus, what I believe we need is a faith (1) that science can indeed bring about complete agreement on factual belief about human behavior, (2) that such agreement in factual belief will relatively soon result in agreement in attitudes held by people, and (3) that resultantly a continuous adaptation of values to the society's ever-changing needs will eventually effect the directed reconstruction of all social institutions (Dewey, 1948, p. xxiii).

In closing this Section Three, what has been stated immediately above about the relationship between science and changing values is typically occurring already despite the efforts of many to hold back the hands of time. In Section Four, immediately following, you will be presented with "a way out of ethical confusion"--if that indeed is the present state you are in. This will be the introduction of a "interim," three-step approach that will help you move smoothly from a "commonsense" approach to one that represents a solid beginning. Let us proceed.

SECTION IV
A Way Out of Ethical Confusion

In this Section Four. a three-step, philosophic approach to ethical decision-making (i.e., from the thought of Kant to Mill to Aristotle) will be recommended for your study and application **first**--as an *initial* approach to ethical decision-making.[1] This recommendation is based on the assumption that you haven't already adopted one or the other of the more advanced approaches to ethical decision-making.) When you are confronted with an ethical problem in life that needs resolution--whether such a situation arises in your personal or professional life (both are "personal," of course), you may not recognize it as an ethical one at first. One's first reaction is to say (perhaps implicitly to oneself), "What should I do?" Note that "should" always applies to issues and problems of an ethical nature, unless the situation also has legal or quasi-legal ramifications. If so, then it typically becomes "What must I do?" as well.

The First Half of the 20th Century

By now you may agree that there are almost as many views of moral philosophy and/or ethics as there are philosophers (an obvious exaggeration, of course). However, checking on this observation soon leads one to a conviction that there is no single, non-controversial foundation stone upon which the whole structure of ethics can be built. In fact, it can even be argued that the nature and function of the subject are themselves subject to vigorous dispute. This is not to say, however, that there are not some aspects of this branch of philosophy upon which there is fairly wide agreement. In mid-20th century Nowell-Smith (1954), for example, pointed out that earlier moral philosophers sought to offer general guidance about (1) what to do, (2) what to seek, and (3) how to treat others. As we begin the twenty-first century, such guidance from the "mother discipline" is but a distant memory for old-timers.

Earlier philosophers as a rule did not try to preach to their adherents in the same way as theologians did, although many made strong efforts to offer practical advice that included pronouncements on the subject of good and evil. Many early philosophers did believe that there could (should) be a true moral code--i.e., a normative ethical system upon which people could and should base their conduct. In this sense, therefore, philosophers saw their mission as the enunciation of basic principles of morality along with the provision of supporting justification. What is good? What is the good life? What are the limits of moral justification? How shall people live their lives? These were the types of questions to which philosophers spoke.

Others in society have, of course also offered advice to the public. Theologians, dramatists, novelists, poets, and even comedians have offered considerable insight into the question of good and evil. However, such counsel was often characterized as pronouncements or dicta. It was usually different from distinctly philosophic accounts in that it was specific, unsystematic, and typically lacking in proof.

As mentioned previously, there has been strong disagreement with the traditional conception of the philosopher's task. Some believed that philosophers should not, or could not, discover new truths (e.g., Kant), while others felt just the opposite to be the case (e.g., Bentham). Down through the ages, there has been an effort to systematize the knowledge that humans already have and to demonstrate the ultimate rationale for these beliefs. Some were concerned with objective justification of any moral claims, whereas others (known as subjectivists) argued that true objectivity was neither possible nor reasonable.

As a result of these two diametrically opposed positions, one group was extremely skeptical about any body of knowledge that purported to tell people how they should live. Their opposition, the objectivists, worked away toward the achievement of their goal--the creation of a true moral code. In this struggle, the German iconoclast, Nietzsche, was a true revolutionary in that he contradicted previous objectivist thought violently, including even the commonsense moral principles unchallenged by most skeptics. In summary, therefore, the battle lines were quite sharply drawn: one group of ethical theorists agreed with what was presumably the traditional task of the philosopher (i.e., finding a true code), while the other (the subjectivists) denied that moralists could ever hope to achieve such a truly justifiable moral code.

The Second Half of the 20th Century

It is difficult, but not impossible, to gain some historical perspective on the philosophical trends and developments in the second half of the twentieth century. What is now called "the analytic movement" (or "philosophical analysis" or "analytic philosophy") has taken over largely. It has been an interesting and most important development in the English-speaking world at least during the present era. However, despite the fact that scholars in the Western world have been engaged in philosophical thought for more than 2000 years, there is still controversy over the exact nature of philosophy (i.e., what it is and what it should be). And so into the earlier struggle between the ethical objectivists and the ethical subjectivists came a third combatant, the contemporary "analytic" philosopher of the twentieth century. In retrospect, it seems fair to say that this person was one who asked, "What kind of an activity am I engaging in?"

Searching for the answer to this question in the first half of the century, philosophers of this persuasion developed three different approaches (or methodologies) that became known as (1) logical atomism, (2) logical positivism, and (3) ordinary language philosophy. Each looked at analysis somewhat differently, but there was agreement that philosophy must be approached through the medium of language analysis--to a greater or lesser extent. Logical atomists sought to rearrange our ambiguous language so that more logically arranged sentences would become crystal clear. The goal of the logical positivist was to subject statements to a verifiability principle. This meant that regular language statements were to be arranged in logical, consistent form to discover if they were empirically verifiable either through mathematical reasoning or scientific investigation. Finally, the main goal of what was called ordinary language philosophy was to decide what the basic philosophical terms were, and then to use them correctly and precisely so that all might understand. Obviously, these developments had some relationship to the position of the ethical subjectivists, but were a far cry from the efforts of the ethical objectivists seeking to find the one true moral code.

Finally, in the fourth quarter of the twentieth century, the specter of the unknown new century was looming directly ahead on the horizon in a world characterized by "hot and cold" wars and struggles. And what did we find at the very time when people of all ages are highly concerned about changing morality and ethical standards (i.e., about "what to do, what to seek, and how to treat others")? Simply put, we found brilliant philosophers, the large majority of whom are silent on any answers to these basic questions. They simply avoid the rational (public) justification of any type of moral system. Instead they spend their professional time and energy analyzing the meaning and function of moral concepts and statements or some other so-called analytic approach to the doing of philosophy. (Fairly often, also, the thoughts of some long-dead philosopher are brought to light again resulting in revisionist conjecture!) The end result is an enormous chasm between traditional normative ethics of the avowed moral philosopher and the analytic (or critical or theoretical) approach of that branch of ethics now known as metaethics.

If the above sounds critical of those who pursue such an intensive analytic approach to the detriment of more "people-based" philosophizing, I will have achieved my purpose here. However, in the same breath, I repeat my earlier thought that careful analysis is necessarily important in any philosophical undertaking. Thus, I have an obligation to explain what I think the relationship should be between normative ethics and metaethics. For example, if I may use an instance from a subject I know well (i.e., competitive sport), people involved professionally in sport--whether they know it or not--need metaethical advice from philosophers on the concept of "violence." Moreover, the need is equally as important for the development of codes of ethical conduct for professional coaches and professional athletes. Such codes involving normative statements could provide important guidance at a time when firm counsel seems absolutely necessary.

By the above statements, I trust that I have made clear that I don't for a moment wish to imply that metaethical analysis is unimportant--far from it. Obviously, as is always the case, there are extremists on both sides of this question. A more reasonable approach--and there has been movement in this direction recently--would be one in which an ethical theorist (a moral philosopher, if you will) engages in metaethical analysis if he or she wishes, and as necessary. However, at the same time he or she also works toward the elimination of irrational ethical beliefs while searching for as much normative consensus as possible.

For the field of philosophy to work for such general agreement to the extent possible, a normative consensus if you will, is vitally important at this time as the public struggles with a search for the "best" ethical system consonant with an evolving democratic society. A variation of this might be a situation where university departments of philosophy would deliberately engage scholars with strong inclinations in one direction or the other, the end result of which would tend to strengthen both the sub-disciplinary and subprofessional aspects of the field (i.e., those branches concerned with both the metaethical and normative aspects of philosophy). It is my feeling that the public, in the final analysis, would really appreciate the end result.

Following up on the above "pronouncement," I do nevertheless recognize, as you, the reader, may also recognize shortly, that the task of normative inquiry can be most difficult. And, admittedly, this is especially so when people are confronted with most complex personal and social issues, and their conclusions tend to stray into the realm of metaethics. For example, when a normative ethical theory such as hedonism (the position that a person's primary moral duty lies in the pursuit of pleasure) includes a statement such as "Going to church is good because it brings pleasure to the parishioner." In response, the non-hedonist might challenge this statement solely on the meaning of the terms "good" and "pleasure." The obvious difficulty of justifying a normative ethical theory brings to the fore questions about metaethical relativism and subjectivism, questions which when pursued carefully point up the validity of the "subjectivist threat."

In summary, I have sought to explain that historically we have no single, non-controversial foundation stone for the entire structure of ethics. Yet we are finding that ever more difficult ethical questions are being asked as the world grows increasingly complex. Here I have explained that early philosophers attempted to provide both answers and advice to life's many problems. But today, sadly as I see it, ethical advice--dubious or otherwise--comes from any and all sources. The fact that precious little comes to help "ordinary" people from trained philosophers today is, as I see it, a tragedy. Thus, I argue that we need a much-improved balance between the attention paid by philosophers to normative ethics and that given to metaethics. I will strive to offer the reader such "balance" as we move ahead here.

Basically, then, justification of an ethical theory, or even an incomplete set of ethical statements about any aspect of life, revolves around the ability of the theorist to state correctly, explain sufficiently, and defend adequately his or her ethical claims and arguments. Is your ethical statement objective or subjective? In what way does an ethical judgment differ from a factual judgment? Is any ethical statement about right or wrong conduct in any life situation "publicly warrantable"? In other words, is there some publicly acceptable procedure for verification, a procedure that intelligent, reasonable people would be willing to accept?

Finally, then, as you move ahead with this "ethical experience," you must decide for yourself to what extent you personally want ethical claims or judgments to be (1) objectively verifiable (capable of being proved)1, (2) universalizable (acceptable worldwide), (3) practical for use in everyday life, and (4) autonomous in the sense that the structure of the statements comprising the claim or judgment--its very fabric--does not solely on non-normative statements (i.e., theoretical explanations). (You may not appreciate it yet here, but--both personally and professionally--this experience with ethical decision-making could well be extremely important to you in the years that lie ahead.

So please read on. . . .

Three Philosophers

Here in Section Four, I am first going to call upon the name and ideas of three philosophers. I am referring to Immanuel Kant, John Stuart Mill, and the ancient Greek philosopher, Aristotle. I am recommending that you experiment with this three-step approach first. I came to believe that some of their basic thought on ethical matters--not all, by any means--provides an easy and "palatable" entrance into this subject for most people--in this culture at least.

You may think that I am encouraging you to become a philosophical charlatan or sophist because it's the simplest way to get at a difficult subject. However, let me hasten to state that I have great respect for each of these men and the contributions that each one of them has made to the history and development of philosophy. Of course, as is the case always, no person is perfect nor has perfect knowledge either. However, the influence of each has been great and merits recognition for a variety of reasons. I must admit also that, as a creature of Western culture. their ideas have considerable appeal to me despite my strong inclination to adopt a scientific ethics approach only as we move ahead in the 21st century.

The progression of major ideas to be presented moves from certain underlying principles that each has presented. It occurred to me initially that it might be helpful to draw an analogy with the sport of baseball. Thus, I originally decided to call the first phase (Phase One) of this overall plan of "ethical attack" by what is considered to be one of the most skillful and fortuitous maneuvers in baseball, the triple play.

From Tinkers to Evers to Chance was an early combination of shortstop, second baseman, and first baseman in baseball in the execution of a double play. So, in a sense, I began earlier by initially suggesting that you, the reader, proceed from Kant to Mill to Aristotle to complete a triple play. But then, Don Morrow, a colleague, argued that these three baseball players were really a double-play combination (i.e., by their typical maneuver only two players were declared out). To make it a triple play, the first named player would have to catch a line drive (one out!) and then would have to throw to two different bases to make outs No. 2 and No. 3. At any rate, it all got too confusing, and I have now named it a three-step approach--from Kant (test of consistency) to Mill (test of **net** consequences) to Aristotle (test of intentions).

In other words, when you are confronted with the need or desire to make an ethical decision in your life, the conclusion you draw--or the course of action you plan to take--should be able to withstand the three tests of this approach. In the pages that follow, then, each of these three steps will be discussed in some detail.

> (**Note**: Later I will show the strong similarity of these three steps to the layout devised by philosopher Stephen Toulmin for the construction of a sound jurisprudential argument that could stand up in a court of law. By this means [i.e., Toulmin's approach] you would be able to lend further support--or possibly discredit!--whatever conclusion you had reached initially with the ethical problem or issue at hand.)

Kant's Test of Consistency (Step 1)

Without going into any detail about Kant's overall position, it should be explained that he did distinguish sharply between what might be called naturalistic ethics and moral law. His "categorical imperative" implied a moral code above and beyond any law of nature (e.g., above the human's strong desire for gratification and happiness). Basically, he postulated a universalizability criterion as the most fundamental moral principle. It is this that we are using for Step 1 or the test of consistency (or universalizability). In other words, you should "act only on that maxim which you can will to be a universal law."

The similarity between this dictum and our culture's Golden Rule is, of course, immediately apparent. Kant's more precise statement of the "golden rule" may well in time be viewed as his greatest contribution to the subject of ethics (despite what some people immediately draw to our attention as its obvious weaknesses). For example, George Bernard Shaw's cryptic retort to this admonition was: "Don't do unto others as you would have them do to you--their tastes might be different." Also, Kaufmann (1973) felt that the negative formulation of the Golden Rule was far superior to the original, but that it too had serious deficiencies (p. 188). Further, in an ABC television political discussion (Jan. 16, 1983), George Will quipped, "Do unto others as fast as they do unto you." So it is true that there are maxims that could not be universalized, and also that there are ones that it might not be desirable to universalize. Thus, we must ask ourselves by what criterion (or criteria) are we to tell which maxim should be universalized. (By "universalizability" is meant, of course, whether it would be possible or desirable to extend an action to include all people on earth.)

To help you to get over this first major hurdle, I recommend the introduction of a number of subprinciples at this point, subprinciples that are based on the espoused values of North American culture. The late Michael Bayles (1981, p. 5) had suggested that we can turn to the chief values for help in our acceptance of ethical norms. So, when you attempt to implement the test of consistency to an ethical decision that you make (or intend to make), or perhaps encourage another to make, the following are a number of questions that you could well ask yourself (phrased negatively; see Fox & DeMarco, 1990, p. 174) :

1. Would my action or decision (or inaction) impose on another's freedom?
2. Would my action hurt another person?
3. Would my action impose on an individual's privacy?
4. Would my action deny an opportunity to another person?
5. Would my action be against the law?
6. Would my action be unfair?
7. Would my action be hurtful to another's welfare?

Then, assuming that you can answer, with reasonable assurance, all of these questions negatively, you are ready to proceed to Step 2.

Mill's Test of (Net) Consequences (Step 2)

Step 2 of our approach has been selected from the heritage of philosophic utilitarianism. For the maxim "Act so as to bring about the greatest good possible," we are in debt to John Stuart Mill, as well as another important early philosopher, Jeremy Bentham. Here we are recommending that you invoke what may be called a "test of (net) consequences"--that is, assessing what the total effect of your action (or inaction) would be. Also, you should keep in mind that our concern here is with the promotion of the maximum amount of *net*, not *gross*, happiness. *In other words, try to weigh the good that would be done, the bad that would be done, and then determine whether more good than bad would be the end result.*

At this point, once again, such thoughts come to mind as whether an action is fair, just, or beneficent, and also permits autonomy on the part of the other person(s) involved. Note that these criteria are the same (e.g., fair, harmful) as the questions raised in Step 1 above. Thus, we should determine what the best available evidence tells us. Additionally, recall that with ethical considerations we are dealing with the concepts of good and bad, and right and wrong. Here Mill's (1861) famous definition answering the question "What is wrong?" can be of help:

> We do not call anything wrong, unless we mean to imply that a person ought to be punished in some way or other for doing it; if not by law, by the opinion of his fellow creatures; if not by opinion, by the reproaches of his conscience. This seems to be the real turning point of the distinction between morality and simple expediency (Utilitarianism, V).

What then is the logic of this second step we are offering for your use in this initial three-step approach? Kalish and Montague (1964) offered the following formal definition: "An argument is valid if it is possible for its premises to be true and its conclusions false" (p. 3). Well and good; however, one is apt to say "Huh?" at first reading of this statement. So let's try something like, "If all the premises are true, then the conclusion will be true." Using basic *modus ponens* logic from traditional philosophy, then, the following premises and conclusion apply in this instance:

1. The act that--on the basis of the best evidence available at the time of acting--produces the greatest total good is right.
2. This act will produce the great total good.
3. Therefore, this act is right (*modus ponens*)

Act-Utilitarianism. This, then, is the basic utilitarian approach for what has subsequently been called act-utilitarianism. (A second utilitarian approach named *rule-utilitarianism* will be described in the note immediately below.)

"So far, so good," you may be saying, "this second step seems quite simple compared to the first step recommended." Unfortunately, this is not quite true, because a number of questions may be raised to show that--as usual!--things are never as simple as they seem to be at first glance. For example, suppose that you had made a solemn promise to your best friend, and suddenly you realize that by keeping that promise you won't be doing the most good?

Or, to consider another problematic situation, suppose you have a son who had turned out to be worthless. However, you also have a really intelligent, hardworking nephew. Assuming that both of them want to go to college, and that both need financial assistance, should you help your nephew before your own son on the assumption that you could do more good that way?

Or, to make the topic even more complex, the archetypic example of the dilemma that one might be facing as a strict act-utilitarian might be as follows: You are living in the family home with your crippled father, a wonderful old person. To help with finances, you have taken in a roomer, a brilliant, young cancer researcher. One evening you return home very late, and you find your home ablaze. Realizing that both your father and the young researcher are probably asleep on the second floor, whom do you attempt to rescue first?

> (**Note**: *Rule-Utilitarianism.*. There is a second type of utilitarianism known as rule-utilitarianism that is not being recommended here. You might find this more appealing than the approach just described. With this approach you are admonished not to judge the rightness of an act by the act's consequences. Now you are to judge the rightness or wrongness of an act by the consequences of adopting the rule under which the particular act falls. Following the consequences of a rule instead of a particular act often colors a problematic situation markedly. One reason for this, of course, is that it is often extremely difficult to find the best rule!)

There are undoubtedly arguments that you can think of to show that this second step, the test of consequences, is not infallible no matter whether you base your actions on the consequences of an individual act. Nevertheless, the test of consistency (or universalizability) first, and then this test of consequences, at least offer a person some criteria infinitely better than mere common sense upon which to proceed when one is confronted with the need to make the best possible ethical decision under a given set of circumstances.

Aristotle's Test of Intentions (Step 3)

Step 3 of the this approach to ethical decision-making we may call the test of intentions. For this sage advice we turn to the ancient Greek philosopher, Aristotle (the tutor of Alexander the Great). In his

Nicomachean Ethics (Loomis, 1943) Aristotle asked, "What were the conditions under which the act was performed?" Virtue, as defined by Aristotle, "is concerned with emotion and action, and emotions and actions that are voluntary are objects for praise or blame, while those that are involuntary are objects for pardon and sometimes for pity" (p. 113). Aristotle's point here is that, in a study of virtue, it is essential to know whether a person's actions were voluntary or involuntary. (Of course, such knowledge is still most important when considering judgment in a court of law today.) Aristotle understood that such consideration was important for lawmakers and judges (e.g., an act carried out under compulsion or ignorance could be considered involuntary and perhaps pardonable).

A very practical example of these ideas would be a situation where a person has committed a crime (e.g., murder). Obviously (invoking Step 1 of our recommended three-step approach), we certainly would not wish to see such an act "universalized" and carried out against all people on earth. Further, this particular act of murder had most serious consequences (Step 2) and did not contribute to the greatest (net) good or happiness of anyone. In fact, the opposite was the case! Yet, if we wish to judge this seemingly heinous crime as good, bad, or neutral, *Aristotle would argue that we need to know under what conditions the act was carried out.*

For example, we read in the newspaper occasionally that someone has done harm to, or killed, another person who has earlier committed a major crime against the current attacker's relative (e.g., sexual assault). In such cases we might feel that justice had been done even though a law was broken in so doing. Or, depending on the specific circumstances, we might even feel sorry for the original perpetrator of the crime upon whom revenge had subsequently been carried out. Thus, even though this person (i.e., the original wrongdoer in this instance) had committed what we would call a major crime, we might still feel sympathetically inclined to him or her because we owed this person a personal debt of gratitude (or perhaps because we had been close friends in the past).

And, as it happens, the question of the intentions of the person who commits what is determined to be a wrong is evident typically when a law court considers a case of murder. A premeditated case of murder is called first-degree murder, whereas a so-called crime of passion (i.e., seemingly instinctive action) that results in the death of another may be identified as second-degree murder and presumably less blameworthy. Further, if someone accidentally kills another by hitting him with an automobile in a street accident, this is usually designated as manslaughter (person slaughter today?). Finally in this vein, we have read about the extremely low percentage of convictions in Italy when a husband commits murder in the case of his wife's accused lover. Evidently in certain countries many feel this is justifiable homicide! However, this does not typically apply in the case of a wife who kills the "other" woman.

Finally, in relation to Step 3 (test of intentions), or behavior motivation, Aristotle stated that people acted according to one or more of the following reasons: chance, nature, compulsion, habit, reason, passion, and desire. Considering this proposed list, however, leads one to conclude that there are indeed some acts where it is questionable whether an act is indeed voluntary or involuntary. When such doubt arises, Aristotle called such an act one of "mixed character." Some actions, then, "are voluntary, although in the abstract they may be called involuntary, because no one would choose any such act in itself" (p. 114).

Developing a Legal Argument to Back the Three-Step Plan

Recall that there were three sequential steps (tests to apply)--that is, proceeding from Kant to Mill to Aristotle so as to assess (1) consistency (universalizability), (2) consequences, and (3) intentions. Now I am introducing a "verification process" for your consideration.

You could get by (i.e., achieve a reasonably satisfactory result) in the making of ethical decisions with the three-step approach only. This verification process can (should?) be employed as possible to strengthen your decision. It happened that the three initial steps (1, 2, and 3) of the first phase can be quite neatly superimposed on a "reinforcement mechanism" for your phase-one decision. So now I am introducing what Stephen Toulmin (1964) called his "layout for a jurisprudential argument" (p. 95).

Interestingly, Toulmin's approach is a formally valid argument in proper form that is similar to arguments employed daily in law (jurisprudence) and mathematics. As he explains, it is "laid out in a tidy and simple geometrical form" (p. 95). At this point I will simply introduce the "bare bones" of this argument for illustrative purposes.

Toulmin explained that an argument is like an organism. He then proceeded to designate the "chief anatomical units of the argument--its 'bodily organs,' so to speak" (p. 94 et ff.). After assessing it carefully, you will see that his logical apparatus (i.e., the logical form of a valid argument as one in which there is a combination of a formal, procedural argument in proper form with a straightforward, elementary geometrical design) has considerable merit for use in everyday personal and professional ethical decision-making.

Step 1: From Data to Conclusion. You should understand that this Toulmin's argument (with *four* steps) is not being presented as formal logic in which D (Data) *by definition* leads us to C (Conclusion). In other words, this is not what logicians call a *modus ponens* situation in formal logic. It is simply the beginning of a rational argument that one might expect to hear in a court of law any day of the week. You are basically being asked to move forward gradually, steadily, and reasonably from D to C, from the data (D) to what appears to be a reasonable conclusion (C). In this particular example, taken from commercialized intercollegiate athletics in the United States, these initial steps might appear as follows:

D (DATA)	SO	C (CONCLUSION)
A head coach in the U.S. is in a position to exercise undue interpersonal power over recruited, subsidized athletes		Universities should act so as to control the potential for undue use of such power

Power here is defined by Wilson (1978) as "the ability or official capacity to exercise control or influence over others" (p. 303)--that is the leverage that the coach can apply in regard to whether an athlete takes stimulants, painkillers, or bodybuilding agents regularly to improve performance. What are the sources of this power? Actually, there are at least nine different ways that a head coach in these circumstances might employ the interpersonal power that he or she has at hand, elements that I believe should be employed very carefully *if at all.*

Examples of these "sources of power" are the concepts of love and fear, either of which might be a feeling that the athlete has for his or her coach. Either of these sources can be overt or subtle, and is often irrational. A third source of interpersonal power that could well place the coach in too strong a position vis a vis the athlete is that the athlete may have too strong a desire, or too pressing a need, to make the grade athletically. This list has been extended to at least nine sources (Zeigler, 1984, pp. 245-248).

(**Note**: At this point, because it is often necessary to convey different degrees of intensity or force, you will need to introduce-- i.e., make use of--a qualifying term immediately prior to the statement of your conclusion (e.g., necessarily, presumably, probably, under "x" condition). All of this makes the development of a valid argument more difficult and complex, of course, but not unreasonably so. This qualifier is needed because any such distinction or qualifier will affect the import of the conclusion (C) that may be drawn. For example, in the argument that has been developed thus far about the head coach, I might ask myself whether D (data) necessarily [interpreted as needfully or essentially] leads to C (conclusion). This question could be answered affirmatively even more strongly after the introduction of Step 2 below, the warrant.)

This qualifying term, called the Modal Qualifier (Q) by Toulmin, obviously helps to both clarify and make more complex the nature of the argument. Q relates to C; yet, it is distinct from it in that it speaks about W's [the warrant's] "ability" to sound authoritative (or not) about the relationship between D and C. In this example, I have been bold enough to recommend that the modal qualifier (Q) should be interpreted to mean "necessarily" [thus viewed as needful or essential].)

I reason that I can be so forceful, because I firmly believe that, over the years of the 20th century, there has developed a truly substantive body of evidence of all types indicating that both coaches and athletes have been subjected to great pressures. A great variety of rules and regulations have been promulgated by the many athletic conferences in an effort to keep athletics "educational," whatever that may mean today. And yet we find conditions are no better now at the turn of the 21st century than they were in 1929 when a starkly condemnatory report was published. This confirms to me that in many instances the situation is truly "out of hand." I actually believe that conditions are so out of hand that it is questionable whether any person, group of persons, or institution can do anything to remove the evil that exists. Therefore, this is my rationale for using the modal qualifier (Q) necessarily. (Please see Step 2 of Phase Two immediately below where "Q" has been introduced.)

Step 2: The Warrant. Step 2 in the Toulmin argument layout involves the creation of "general hypothetical statements," which can act as "bridges," and thereby authorize the sort of step to which our particular argument commits us (p. 98). Such a statement is called the Warrant (W) so that it may be distinguished from both Data (D) and Conclusion (C). A warrant may be explained further as a sanction, justification, practical standard, canon or argument, value, or norm. So, on our way to the conclusion of the argument started in Step 1, I am now asking you to add a warrant (a "How do you get there justification?" if you will) to the basic question mandated initially--"What conclusion might you draw from the facts on hand?" (i.e., the Conclusion [C] derived from the Data [D]).

With the present argument, therefore, the warrant (W) could be a statement such as "In a democratic society it is considered morally wrong to use another person as a means to an end entirely or largely through the employment of exploitation, deception, and/or treachery." If I were now to symbolize the relationship among the three elements introduced to this point (i.e., D, W, and C), it could look as follows:

      D   SO, (Q   C

    SINCE
      W

Or, to carry the present example through Step 2:

      D   SO (Q)   C

A head coach in the U.S.   Universities
is in a position to exer-   should act so as
cise undue interpersonal   to control the
power over recruited,   potential for
subsidized athletes   undue use of such
                                                                     power in this country

    SINCE
      W

In a democratic society it
is considered wrong to use
another person unduly as a means
to an end entirely or largely
through the employment of

exploitation, deception, and/
or treachery

The warrant here is designated as "incidental and explanatory," its function "being simply to register explicitly the legitimacy of the steps involved and to refer it back to the larger class of steps whose legitimacy is being presupposed" (p. 100). Thus, warrants are general, but data are specific. Warrants are used--but rarely called by that name--in all aspects of life, including people's occupations. Quite simply, they help us to judge on a rational basis any ideas or arguments we may encounter daily.

Step 3: Rebuttal (Or Condition of Exception). Step 3, which has been called the Rebuttal (R) (or Condition of Exception), has a relationship to the warrant, also, because it may influence the strength of the warrant markedly. In fact the rebuttal (R), or condition of exception, can offer particular circumstances of greater or lesser import that might negate or even refute the authority of the warrant (W). However, I must be careful to characterize the degree of force or intensity that each rebuttal (R) can exert on the conclusion (C) being drawn. For example, some coaches in highly commercialized programs seem to be arguing for complete freedom of action as they use the "survival of the fittest" argument put forth by Plato (1961) in the Gorgias (p. 73). However, I would be inclined to call such an individual either psychopathic or megalomaniacal.

In Step 3, therefore, the relationship--to this point--among a total of five elements (D, Q, C, W, and R) can be symbolized as follows:

D	SO, (Q)	C
SINCE		UNLESS
W		R

Or carrying the present argument through Step 3 literally, it might look something like the following:

D	SO (Q)	C
A head coach in the U.S. is in a position to exercise undue interpersonal power over recruited, subsidized athletes		Universities should control undue use of such power in this country

SINCE	UNLESS
W	R
In a democratic society it is considered wrong to use another person as a means to an end entirely or largely through the employment of exploitation, deception, and/or treachery	1. Athlete is actually not hurt by use of such power 2. Athlete doesn't believe he/she is being used 3. Athlete is not unhappy about being used 4. Coach didn't fully appreciate extent to which he/she was using athlete 5. Coach was pressured inordinately to win 6. Society sees no great harm being done and is unwilling to curb what seems to be undue use of such power

Step 4: Backing. In Step 4, the final step in the "rounding out" of the argument that I have been developing, we return to a further consideration (i.e., an extension) of the nature of a warrant. The warrant, as explained in Step 2, is a general, hypothetical, bridge-like statement used to authorize or justify the conclusion being drawn on the basis of the data (evidence) on hand. Recall that the warrant used here explained that it is wrong in this society to use a person through some form of exploitation, deception, and/or treachery.

Despite what has been said above, an inquiry should be made as to the applicability of the warrant as stated in *all* cases in a democratic society. This is why some possible conditions of rebuttal or exception (R)--and also some possible delineations of the coach's intentions are listed. (The question of intentions will be treated below shortly.)

One condition of rebuttal (R) points out that North American society seems unwilling to curb the undue use of interpersonal power by the coach. This argument may also be placed in another context altogether (for the sake of this discussion in a different society or culture). This warrant may actually be relevant and applicable in what is called the Western world. Further, I should also ask to what extent it would be relevant and applicable in all countries in other cultures. Of course, I hope it is most relevant and applicable there too, but then I need to ask additionally if society "looks the other way" there too--as it seems to do all to often in the United States especially.

At any rate, in Step 4 my aim is to present the idea of providing Backing (B) for the warrant that I choose to use in developing the pattern or layout for this jurisprudential argument. Here the backing (B) supplements or strengthens the warrant even further. Thus, I state that the strength of the warrant becomes even greater when it is appreciated that the use of interpersonal power through exploitation, deception, and/or treachery involves *entrapment* and *manipulation* as well! As a result it is now possible to add the following backing (B), preceded by the words "On account of," to strengthen the warrant (W) even further: "The written and unwritten rules and laws of society. Manipulation of this type usually involves deception (or even coercion) to which there is a moral reaction because of the effort to control or elicit behavior through interference with another's operative goals and thereby to destroy or seriously damage his/her personal dignity."

Invoking the additional Step 4 completes the presentation of the recommended layout to be employed in the ethical analysis of a *jurisprudential* argument. Of course, it is recognized that there is a "field-dependence" for backing of this type (i.e., it matters a great deal whether one is dealing with the subject of ethics, the discipline of physics, or the profession of law, to name three areas of human involvement). It might have been sufficient simply to state the warrant (W) and leave it at that without adding the backing (B). As Toulmin explained, "the warrant itself is more than a repetition of these facts; it is a general moral of a practical character, about the ways in which we safely argue in view of these facts"(p. 106). Finally in this second phase of the pattern of argument that began as "D, *so* C," it ought to be possible to reverse the structure and move from right to left, or "C, ***because*** D."

In Step 4, then, a sixth element called backing (B) has been introduced. Thus, D, Q, C, W, B, and R are all worked into the presentation of the complete argument and are symbolized as follows:

D　　　　　　　　SO, (Q)　　　　　　　　C

SINCE	UNLESS
W	R
ON ACCOUNT OF	
B	

Or, to carry the argument forward in detail through the final Step 4:

D	SO (Q)	C
A head coach in the U.S. is in a position to exercise undue interpersonal power over recruited, subsidized athletes		Universities should control undue use of such power in this country
SINCE		UNLESS
W		R
In a democratic society it is considered wrong to use another person as a means to an end entirely or largely through the employment of exploitation, deception, and/or treachery		1. Athlete is actually not hurt by use of such power
2. Athlete doesn't believe he/she is being used
3. Athlete is not unhappy about being used
4. Coach didn't fully appreciate the extent to which he/she was using athlete
5. Coach was being pressured inordinately to win
6. Society sees no great harm being done and is unwilling to curb what seems to be undue use of such power
ON ACCOUNT OF		
B		
The written and unwritten rules, regulations, and laws that exist in our society. Such manipulation usually involves deception (or even coercion) to which there is a moral reaction because of the effort to control or elicit		

behavior through interference with
another's operative goals and
thereby to destroy or seriously
damage his/her personal dignity

Key: Jurisprudential Argument Terms:

D = Data (A statement of a situation that prevails in-
 cluding evidence, elements, sources, samples of facts)
Q = Modal Qualifier (adverbs employed to qualify conclusions
 based on strength of warrants (e.g., necessarily, probably)
C = Conclusion (claim or conclusion that we wish to establish)
W = Warrant (practical standards or canons of argument designed
 to provide an answer to the question, "How do you get there?")
B = Backing (categorical statements of fact that lend further
 support to the bridge-like warrants)
R = Conditions of Exception (arguments of rebuttal or exception
 that tend to refute or "soften" the strength of the conclusion)

Summary

In bringing Section IV to a close, I should explain that the utilitarian theory of punishment (i.e., assessment of consequences) is retributive in nature--that is, an offender against the prevailing ethical mores deserves to be punished according to the severity of the crime committed. Most Western societies have advanced beyond the Old Testament's "eye for an eye" dictum. Nevertheless, for example, a thief in Iran may still have his hand cut off. Also, changing times have brought about many cries for the return of capital punishment in countries where the death penalty had been abolished (especially for terrorists, police killers, etc.).

A generation ago, John Rawls (1971) presented a significant conception of "justice as fairness." This was considered by some as a "rescue effort" for what has been called distributive justice. Shortly thereafter, however, Walter Kaufmann argued that distributions can never be just no matter how carefully we might try. In his *Without Guilt and Justice: From Decidophobia to Autonomy*, he attempted to lead us one step farther away from both retributive and distributive justice. Explaining that he envisioned four cardinal virtues (i.e., honesty, courage, "humbition" (i.e. a fusion of ambition with humility), and love , involving the sharing of plights of others), he stated that a person's life goal should be what he called "creative autonomy."

As I start to conclude this section. I trust that you will find appealing the initial ethical decision-making (i.e., from Kant to Mill to Aristotle), as well as the further "verification" possibility of superimposing a jurisprudential (law-court) argument on the basic three-step approach. Finally, then, as you move along to Section Five, I am recommending that you approach each ethical decision-making situation with which you may be confronted in what I am calling an "experiential" approach.

Note:

1. The basic three-step approach in this section (i.e., proceeding from the thought of Kant to that of Mill, and finally to that of Aristotle) was recommended by **Professor Richard Fox, Cleveland State University** as a viable initial method of ethical decision-making for undergraduate university students. I have amplified it somewhat with various "sub-principles" and then I also superimpose the "approach" on Toulmin's "layout for a jurisprudential argument." Professor Fox should not be "responsible" for any subsequent additions in this plan after the original approach (i.e., moving from Kant to Mill to Aristotle, etc.). *I did want to make certain, however, that he was recognized for his recommendation of the basic three-step approach used here.*

SECTION FIVE
Examples of the Three-Step Approach to Ethical Decision-Making

In Section Five you will be introduced directly to examples of what I have called ethical decision-making for (1) *personal,* (2) *professional,* and (3) *environmental* problems. The term "environmental," as used here, means problems that humans face because of their role in society at large as citizens (i.e., because of the conditions of Earth itself and various social and political involvements they may have.) Below you will find 6 case situations described and analyzed briefly in both written and tabular form. The analyses are based on the three-step approach described in Section Four. (Each three-step approach to ethical decision-making is superimposed on a jurisprudential [law-court] argument.)

Personal Ethical Decision-Making Problems

Introduction

In analyzing each of these so-called personal decision-making cases, I sought first to determine "who had a duty or responsibility to do what" in each of the cases. I then had to decide whether someone also had an ethical obligation to "do this" or "not to do that" in the situation concerned. As I made this assessment, I kept in mind the following questions about the actions (or inactions) of one or more of the major individuals concerned:

1. Is the action basically unfair to a person or group?
2. Does the action or decision (or inaction) impose on another's freedom
3. Does the action hurt another person's welfare?
4. Does the action impose on an individual's privacy
5. Does the action deny an opportunity to another person?
6. Is the action, in addition to being one of the above, also illegal (thus adding another dimension to the analysis)?

> (**Note:** In the first two cases--those which we are calling examples of *personal* ethics including what has been said immediately above--I was also thinking about the establishment of any or all standards of virtue [e.g., honesty, fairness] in any personal decision-making situation. These would be opposed to the presence of any or all standards of vice [e.g., exhibition of prejudice, action of theft, doing of harm].)

With an ethical obligation, it is best to use the word "should" (i.e., "As her superior, Joe should not taken advantage of Marie when she was in such a vulnerable position").

When the obligation has been accepted as a societal norm--and has subsequently been instituted legally (i.e., "Joe committed a criminal offense when he assaulted Marie sexually after the office had closed for the day")--the "should not" can obviously be further strengthened by "must not".

I also assumed the role of one of the major participants in the case situation, and then made recommendations as to what should be done (ethically)--and what must also be done (legally) if what happened violated both a societal norm and established law.

Now please read on as these "sample situations" are offered for your consideration as to how these three steps may be employed in an everyday situation.

Case 1: "Beth's & Tim's Dilemma"

Beth, who has been accepted for admission next year at the state university, evidently made a serious mistake. She (they) didn't mean to "go all the way" with Tim after a party following the final football game. But it happened; they had a few drinks together, on the spur of the moment made love passionately without protection. Now she has tested positively for pregnancy. Beth hadn't thought too much about it when she missed her period, because she was a very active person and this happened occasionally. To make matters worse, however, Beth has now missed her second period, and the situation is rapidly turning into a real tragedy. Beth and Tim are simply not ready for married life. Beth's parents are heartbroken, and Tim's parents are equally upset. Beth wants an abortion as soon as possible even though such an action is not sanctioned by her religion. But she knows it is legal, and her parents tend to agree reluctantly. But Tim's parents are divided on the subject, and Tim himself is anxious "to do the right thing." He was thinking of attending community college in the fall. So his plans obviously do not include fatherhood at this time. Beth must now decide what to do.

Analysis. This is a highly complex issue at present--and perhaps will always be so in the future. The question of an abortion basically revolves around a decision as to whether a fetus is a person at conception. The Supreme Court's decision in the United States (Roe vs. Wade) brought about a significant change in attitude, but a significant minority of the populace is still most strongly anti-abortion at any point in a pregnancy. The basic question is whether an abortion is a case of murder of a human, or whether the fetus achieves status as a human only in the latter phase of a pregnancy when life is detected in the womb? Or beyond this, should the fetus be considered human only after birth? Suppose, also, for example, that the unborn fetus is defective and would if born become a burden to the parents and to society? Does that make a difference? It must be asked further in any analysis whether the state and/or the church should (or can) have anything to say about such an intimate matter as the health care of a citizen's body. It is obvious that Beth's analysis and subsequent decision will depend upon a number of personal and social factors (See Table 1 below.).

(Note: Keep in mind that Test 1 (Kant), Test 2 (Mill), and Test 3 (Aristotle) are the basic components of the three-step approach. The other headings listed below in each of the six cases are terminology used in connection with Toulmin's jurisprudential (law-court) argument that can be used to check or vett the basic three-step approach recommended.)

Table 1
DIAGRAMMATIC ANALYSIS (ABORTION)
(With the Three-Step Approach [Fox] **Superimposed**
on the Jurisprudential Argument Layout [Toulmin])

D DATA	Q SO, PRESUMABLY	C CONCLUSION
Beth, a high school senior with plans to attend university in the fall, has become pregnant. She and Tim hadn't planned it that way, and now they and their families have conflicting opinions about what to do, if anything, as to Beth's having an abortion. She wants it desperately so that she can get on with her life.		Plans should be made for an early abortion so that Beth can continue with college plans, and Tim can get on with his life as well. There is no reason why their relationship can't continue if that is their mutual wish.
(SINCE W) WARRANT		(UNLESS R) REBUTTAL OR EXCEPTION
Applying the criterion of universality, a mature person should have the right perhaps after advice to make such a basic decision about her body and her future in all circumstances that might arise.		1. Beth, the person concerned, decided that her religious faith was so strong that the dictates of the Church in the matter should prevail.
TEST NO. 1 (KANT) **(universalizability)**		2. The person involved can be convinced (e.g., by Tim, the father) that carrying the fetus to term is the right thing to do, everything considered.
(ON ACCOUNT OF B) BACKING		
The concept of individual freedom		3. Beth, after consideration,

is basic and extremely important as humans search for "the good life" in a world that has in the past so often been beset by tyranny and slavery. Recognition of this individual right in society generally would result in the greatest (net) good or happiness for those involved.

decides to carry the fetus to term and then puts the child up for adoption (thereby not going against her faith and that of her parents).

**TEST No. 3
(ARISTOTLE))
(intentions)**

**TEST No.2 (MILL)
(net consequences)**

Key: Jurisprudential Argument Terms:

D = Data (A statement of a situation that prevails including evidence, elements, sources, samples of facts)
Q = Modal Qualifier (adverbs employed to qualify conclusions based on strength of warrants (e.g., necessarily, probably)
C = Conclusion (claim or conclusion that we wish to establish)
W = Warrant (practical standards or canons of argument designed to provide an answer to the question, "How do you get there?")
B = Backing (categorical statements of fact that lend further support to the bridge-like warrants)
R = Conditions of Exception (arguments of rebuttal or exception that tend to refute or "soften" the strength of the conclusion)

Case 2: "Having It Both Ways"

Bert graduated from community college five years ago and is now a successful insurance salesman. He still lives in the city where he was raised and is active in a number of social and civic organization. He plays both tennis and golf quite well. He has also dated a number of young women, but has never become too serious with any one person. Recently to Bert's surprise, George, a male friend who is a computer programmer became quite friendly and invited Bert over for tennis and dinner on two separate occasions. Bert discovered that he liked George very much and surprised himself by readily acquiescing when he was invited to share a sexual encounter. The following week George called and asked whether Bert might be interested in saving money by moving in with him and sharing expenses in his very nice condo apartment. This new relationship has developed quite suddenly and, as it happens, Bert has also having a semi-serious relationship going with Martha who works in the same office with him. Only last week Bert's mother had invited the couple over for dinner and had made quite a fuss about what a nice person Martha was in a conversation with Bert on the telephone later. Bert is now having fairly strong feelings of guilt about his relationships with both George and Martha. How shall he decide how to handle what has become a highly delicate issue?

Analysis. What Bert does "in the privacy of his own bedroom" is, of course, only Bert's business (although some states still have archaic laws on the books in this regard). However, whether it is fair to have a "relationship" with both friends at the same time must be decided. The "nature vs. nurture" argument arises on the question of homosexuality, but--although evidence is tending in one direction--science has not yet proved definitely that certain genes in a person's make-up are the determining factor in this regard. If Bert were to move in with George, this would definitely be a move in the direction of homosexuality. And it is true that many people still believe strongly that being a homosexual or a lesbian is morally wrong. Also, how would Bert's parents and siblings react to any such move? Further, if the relationship with George became general knowledge, his business interests could well be hurt by the reactions of narrow-minded colleagues or clients. Bert is puzzled, because he would like to keep both relationships intact (i.e., with both George and Martha). Obviously, following this course of action would be most difficult. What should he do?

Table 2
DIAGRAMMATIC ANALYSIS (HOMOSEXUALITY)
(With the Three-Step Approach Superimposed
on the Jurisprudential Argument Layout)

D DATA	Q. SO, LOGICALLY	C CONCLUSION
Bert, a successful insurance salesman living in the community where he grew up, starts a homosexual relationship with George at the same time he has been dating Martha. Now George has asked Bert to move in with		Bert should do some soul-searching and realize that his personal life and professional career may be at stake unless he makes some careful decisions that

him and share condo expenses.
Bert is feeling very guilty
and uncertain about the future,
even though he really is en-
joying both relationships.

(SINCE W)
WARRANT

It is not fair to have a sexual relationship with two different people at the same time in
North American society. Also,
it may be an indication of some
immaturity on Bert's part and
may require some psychological
counseling in the near future.

TEST No.1 (KANT)
(consistency)

(ON ACCOUNT OF B)
BACKING

Prevailing social custom is
such that homosexuality is not
typically accepted, and bi-sexu-
ality is regarded even more
negatively. Unless Bert main-
tains strict secrecy for the time
being, the prevailing situation
could cause great difficulties in
both his social life and professional career.

TEST No.2 (MILL)
(net consequences)

demonstrate fairness to
both Martha & George.
He should seek counsel
from a relative or
friend if available, and
probably from a quali-
fied professional, also.

(UNLESS R)
REBUTTAL OR
EXCEPTION

1. Bert explains the pre-
vailing situation to
both Martha and George,
and each is willing to
permit him a very
short period of time to
make a decision one way
or the other. However,
this may be a dubious
course of action.

2. Bert, after thinking
his predicament over on
his own, decides to
continue his friendship
with George without the
sexual aspect for the
present as he seeks to
sort out his relation-
ship with Martha.

TEST No. 3
(ARISTOTLE)
(intentions)

Key: Jurisprudential Argument Terms:

D = Data (A statement of a situation that prevails in-
    cluding evidence, elements, sources, samples of facts)
Q = Modal Qualifier (adverbs employed to qualify conclusions
    based on strength of warrants (e.g., necessarily, probably)
C = Conclusion (claim or conclusion that we wish to establish)
W = Warrant (practical standards or canons of argument designed
    to provide an answer to the question, "How do you get there?"
B = Backing (categorical statements of fact that lend further
    support to the bridge-like warrants)
R = Conditions of Exception (arguments of rebuttal or exception
    that tend to refute or "soften" the strength of the conclusion)

Professional Ethical Decision-Making Problems

Introduction

With Cases 3 and 4, the emphasis will be primarily on professional ethics. By that I mean that the ethical problems presented here will relate primarily to an individual's relations with others at his or her place of employment. This second (personal &) professional category, therefore, includes two case situations of an ethical nature in which the person is confronted with the need for ethical decision-making in the course of his or her employment as a practicing professional or tradesperson (or as a manager).

Initially, we need to keep in mind that there are values and norms that are basic to life in democratic societies, and that they, accordingly, also relate to the subject matter of ethics. (The term norm here refers to one of a series of standards of virtue that are expected to prevail in this type of society or culture as explained below.) Persons in a responsible world culture can also be expected to be honest, fair, truthful, etc. These are ordinary norms that inevitably also have a relationship to what I call professional norms.

Additionally, over time, certain rights and privileges have been accorded to citizens in democratically oriented countries. In North America, for example, the following norms relating to rights and privileges currently prevail:

1. Governance by law
2. Individual freedom (as much as may be permitted in the social setting)
3. Protection from injury
4. Equality of opportunity
5. Privacy
6. Individual welfare (Bayles, 1981, pp. 5-7).

Second, based on a review of the literature, the following five categories or dimensions are recommended for a code of ethics for a profession (e.g., a teacher ***or any occupation*** that aspires to professional status):

1. The professional's conduct as a teacher

    (The intent here is that the teacher should in the performance of his/her duties, (1) hold paramount the safety, health, and welfare of the public, (2) perform services only in his/her areas of competence, (3) issue public statements only in an objective and truthful manner, (4) act in professional matters for each employer or student/client as faithful agent or trustee, and (5) avoid improper solicitation of professional employment.)

2. The professional's ethical obligations to students/clients

    (The intent here is that the professional should be completely trustworthy and that he/she has the following obligations or responsibilities in his/her relationship with students/clients: To exhibit candor, competence, diligence, discretion, honesty, and loyalty)

3. The professional's ethical responsibility to employers/employing organizations

    (The intent here is that the professional should understand and respect his/her responsibility to both the student/client and third parties [e.g., superior and organization represented] by exhibiting fairness, truthfulness, and non-maleficence [i.e., doing no harm])

4. The professional's ethical responsibility to colleagues/peers and the profession

> (The intent here is that the professional has certain obligations to the profession in regard to doing research; working for reform; providing social leadership; improving professional knowledge and skills; and preserving and enhancing the role of the profession so that society's respect will be maintained.
>
> Under this category, also, the professional should never forget that he/she has an obligation help with the self-regulation of the profession (a) by encouraging desirable young people to enter the profession and (b) by complying with, and seeing to it that others comply with as well, with the established responsibilities and obligations of the profession as explained in the profession's code of ethics)

5. The professional's ethical responsibility to society

> (The intent here is that the professional has an ethical responsibility to society and therefore will make his/her full services available to all who need help regardless of age, sex, physical limitation, ethnic origin, religion, or sexual orientation. Additionally, the professional person will make every effort to see that he/she personally, as well as his/her colleagues, live up to the canons and principles of the profession's code of ethics)

Third, proceeding from Bayles's (1981, Chapters 3-7) categorization of **the basic make-up of any code of ethics** proposed, the progression for the eventual determination of specific rules and regulations moves to a secondary categorization within the heading of professional obligations or responsibilities. Included here **as they might relate to any one of a number of professions** are (a) standards (virtues or vices), (b) principles (where some latitude is possible), and (c) rules that must be adhered to strictly.

Table 3
Examples of Provisions for an Ethical Code
for a Professional Person

Categories	Standards	Principles	Rules
a. Bases upon which professional services are made available	A professional should be fair and just in providing his/her services	A prof. should ensure that all students receive adequate instruction.	A client needing help should receive it as soon as possible

Example: A professional manager shows bias toward a client and manages him/her in a way that might cause the individual--knowingly or unknowingly--to act in wrongful or unethical manner.

Categories	Standards	Principles	Rules
b. Ethical nature of prof.-client relationship	A prof. should be honest in his/her treatment of a client	A prof. should never treat a client as a means to an end	A client must never be forced to take an illegal or unethical action because of fear of loss of status

Example: An athletic director urges an athlete to act in a dishonest or possibly harmful way by stating that the athlete's scholarship will be lost if he doesn't cooperate.

Categories	Standards	Principles	Rules
c. Conflict resolution when conflict arises between prof.'s obligations to clients and third parties	A prof. has an obligation to be truthful in dealing with third parties	In checking a business contract a staff member notices that a few inaccuracies that contravene the earlier verbal agreement made by him on behalf	A staff member must never knowingly permit a client to be taken advantage of in a dishonest manner

of his company

Example: A business salesperson and a client had verbally agreed on certain specifics of an impending contract. When it was time for both parties to formally sign the agreement, several key inaccuracies of such a nature are present that would cheat the client. Somehow they had "crept" into the document.

d. Professional obligations to society,(i.e. dury to serve the public good) and to one's profession	A prof. should be loyal to societal values and those of the profession	A prof. has a duty and responsibility to preserve and enhance the role of the profession in which he/she is a licensed practitioner or symposia annually	A prof. has a duty to upgrade and strengthen his/her knowledge by attending one or more conferences

Example: A professional (in any field) gives the profession a bad name by obviously falling behind on the knowledge in his/her area of expertise to the point that his clients begin to notice it and start looking elsewhere for assistance.

e. Ensuring compliance with the established obligations of the profession's ethical code	A prof. should practice his/her profession with honesty and integrity	A prof. should encourage his/her associates to be honest within the letter and spirit of the established principles and rules of the profession's code of ethics	A prof. who permits his/her colleague to lie or cheat shall be reported and should be excluded from the profession if found guilty

Example: A professional (in any field) who is guilty of unethical practice shall be reported to the ethics committee of the professional society (and subsequently to his/her employers, if such is warranted and/or applicable).

> (**Note:** It should be understood that there always are choices to be made when an individual acts personally or professionally in situations that are less than clear-cut. Thus, if one category is that of obligations (i.e. you must do so-and-so), a second category of available norms may be designated as permissions (i.e. you have freedom of choice because any action may be debatable). In this latter case, professionals are permitted to do (1) what is not prohibited by law; (2) what is not considered unethical in society, generally speaking; and (3) what is not considered to be unethical by the professional society to which one belongs.)

Fourth, and finally then, the listing of eight standards (virtues) should be implemented above in Categories Two and Three (i.e., candor, competence, diligence, discretion, honesty, and loyalty under Category Two; and fairness, non-maleficence, and truthfulness under Category Three). A brief, hortatory, approved ethical creed is typically placed after a preamble to a code of ethics. It remains for a somewhat more detailed code itself to include (a) a listing of the major principles or canons under which the professional person act, and (b) to show how professional associations may begin the process of developing a listing of the specific rules of practice that must be adhered to in daily professional life. (See Table 3 above, also, for a diagrammatic explanation as to how rules of practice can be derived in the immediate future.)

Two characteristic cases in professional ethics will be offered for your consideration. Each case is described briefly, but sufficiently for our purposes here. Then each case is analyzed by implementing the steps followed in Phases One, Two, and Three (see Section Four for a longer explanations of the specific three steps for possible review).

Case 3: "Everybody's Doin' It"

Brad, a college graduate in business administration, obtained a position with responsibility for assisting with the advertising and marketing of his firm's products. His superior, Wesley, appeared to be a real "go-getter." One of the people in the marketing department described him as a person who "wanted to start at the top and work up." Nevertheless, Wes seemed to want to be very helpful to Brad in a number of different ways. Brad was anxious to do well with his new job, of course, and he appreciated the fact that someone was willing to "show him the ropes." As time passed, however, Brad began to perceive that he and Wes were really operating on different wave lengths (so to speak). He told Barbara, his wife, that Wes was really much more realistic and pragmatic than he was. Wes was always trying to cut corners and to get ahead of the other guy (the firm's competitors or even the consumer for that matter). "I guess I'm just too idealistic," Brad said to Barbara one evening during dinner, "but in writing advertising copy I try to tell the truth about our products. They are good, of that I'm certain, but Wes is always on me to write what I feel is dishonest, 'borderline' fraudulent copy." On Barbara's urging, Brad invited Wes out for a beer after work and explained his concerns to him. Wes replied that he knew what Brad was talking about, and he also said that he felt that way once too. "But," he concluded, "I soon learned that the only to get there is to be as 'borderline' as everyone else in this business. It's 'dog-eat-dog' out there, and you simply have to cheat a little here and there and occasionally make wild claims that may not be true--or you'll be left behind in the dust." How should Brad cope with this situation?

Analysis. On the surface the problem faced by Brad in Case 1 seems pretty much "black and white"; either you practice honesty or not. However, as many of us learn along the way, this question can be a highly complex one in numerous life situations encountered. Human relations at the personal level and at the professional level are rarely simple. It is an unfortunate fact that a significant minority of the populace do seem to be ready to cheat or be dishonest in small ways--and at times in more serious ways as well. Then these people of questionable morality tend to rationalize their actions by saying, "Oh, everybody does it; so why shouldn't I?" To permit even minor dishonesty as a "standard" of virtue either in personal or professional life would be fundamentally wrong . Also, if we apply Kant's principle of universality to this matter, it is obvious that everyone doesn't cheat and be dishonest. Secondly, just think of what the net consequences of "everyone doing it" (Mill's principle) would be. It would obviously not be a very nice world in which to live. Lastly, are there situations (Aristotle's thought) where you might be dishonest and yet be moral? Probably very few, although every day we do run into the so-called "white lie" where you may be dishonest in a sense that you lie to someone because you don't want to hurt his or her feelings. And it is true, of course, that a great many people are dishonest in business with their marketing practices when they practice what I call the "We're the greatest!" syndrome even if they know they aren't--if the truth be told. To return to the case at hand, it appears that Brad is going to have to engage in a large measure of soul-searching if he is going to continue and be successful in his present position.

Table 4
DIAGRAMMATIC ANALYSIS (HONESTY)
(With the Three-Step Approach Superimposed
on the Jurisprudential Argument Layout)

D DATA	Q, SO, LOGICALLY	C CONCLUSION
Brad, a business administration major, discovers in his first position in advertising & marketing that his superior is urging him to cut corners and "camouflage" the facts in various ways if he hopes to achieve real success in the advertising game.		Brad will eventually need to decide if he can go along with the morality of the approach that Wes, his superior, says is necessary to succeed in today's "cut-throat" business environment.
(SINCE W) **WARRANT**		**(UNLESS R)** **REBUTTAL** **OR EXCEPTION**
Since the competition in a strongly capitalistic economy even in a democratic state is such that "survival of the fittest" demands that business people follow an aggressive, "borderline" business ethic as they seek to advertise and market their products, businesspeople are being forced to abandon strict application of a code of ethics.		1. Brad can convince himself that it is somehow possible to go along with Wes and still remain true to his principle of honesty and ultimately achieve sufficient success in his career. 2. Brad decides that his youthful idealism about being completely honest in his business dealings was naively idealistic in the realistic business world that he is encountering.
TEST NO. 1 (KANT) **(universalizability)**		**TEST No. 3** **(ARISTOTLE)**

(ON ACCOUNT OF B) **(intentions)**
BACKING

An approach based on communistic theory to the business enterprise, one in which there was a large measure of government ownership and control, has evidently led to waste, corruption, and inefficiency typically; thus, the underlying theory has seemingly not been valid or successful in the long run.

TEST No.2 (MILL)
(net consequences)

Key: Jurisprudential Argument Terms:

D = Data (A statement of a situation that prevails including evidence, elements, sources, samples of facts)
Q = Modal Qualifier (adverbs employed to qualify conclusions based on strength of warrants (e.g., necessarily, probably)
C = Conclusion (claim or conclusion that we wish to establish)
W = Warrant (practical standards or canons of argument designed to provide an answer to the question, "How do you get there?")
B = Backing (categorical statements of fact that lend further support to the bridge-like warrants)
R = Conditions of Exception (arguments of rebuttal or exception that tend to refute or "soften" the strength of the conclusion)

Case 4: Is the "Climate" Better Down South?

    Sam's grandparents and parents have operated a successful garment business in northeastern United States for several generations. This was accomplished by planning, sacrifice, and hard work. They always tried to pay their workers fairly but not exorbitantly. The company's community involvement was such that it was regarded typically as a good "corporate citizen." As time went by, however, the competition increased steadily, and it was difficult indeed to keep the business afloat. The family made every effort to modernize the undertaking, but the profit margin was steadily shrinking despite their best efforts. Local, state, and federal taxes were rising sharply. So the company was forced to go public, but in the final analysis the Bronstein family were only able to retain 40% of the stock shares. Sam's father, who had founded the business originally, was getting close to retirement. He definitely wanted Sam to succeed him before long. In the meantime, the difficulty of making ends meet had forced the workers to complain more seriously than ever before about raises, not to mention the social benefits and the pension plan of the company. Most recently there was a rumor that some of the workers had been lobbying for a vote among the group to establish a union that included a large number of other garment workers in the country. Sam, who had business management education, had seen this move coming for some time, but his father felt somewhat betrayed by "his people" to whom he felt he had always been fair. As the business year was coming to a close, Sam had a long talk with his father. He suggested that, if the group did plan to hold a certification vote, they should start a rumor that it might be time to move the whole enterprise south, perhaps even to Mexico. He thought that perhaps this would cause the vote for a union to fail. If the vote did carry, however, he argued that he would be in favor of following through with the move south anyhow despite the hardship that it would impose on many people and their families. Viewing this ethically, what should Mr. Bronstein and Sam do to keep the business functioning with a reasonable profit? How do you assess Sam approach to the problem?

Analysis. Situations like this have been quite typical in recent years and will undoubtedly continue. Family dynasties with son succeeding father and so on have run into difficulty when conditions forced opening a growing business up to stockholders. The development of unions put a check on rampant capitalism earlier in the century, but the forces of unionism have moved up and down with a spiraling economy. With a capitalistic system, stockholders want a reasonable, if not good, return on their investment. If a business is not showing a good annual return, and it seems like high wages are the culprit, there will be great pressure to move to a locale where salaries and the cost of living are lower. Should Sam do all in his power to defeat the threat of unionism in the family business? Should he, his father, and the extended family forget any responsibility toward hundreds of workers and their families and encourage other stockholders to vote for a change of venue for the factory? Is this the type of action we should seek to "universalize" (Kant) in a democratic society? Is it possible to assess the net consequences (Mill) of a decision one way or the other? How can we weigh the intentions (Aristotle) of the main players in this dilemma?

Table 5
DIAGRAMMATIC ANALYSIS (LOYALTY)
(With the Three-Step Approach Superimposed
on the Jurisprudential Argument Layout)

D DATA	Q SO, LOGICALLY	C CONCLUSION
Sam's family have developed a successful garment business, but for many reasons the profitability margin is down and some stockholders feel it might be necessary to move to a different region of the country. Such a move would put hundreds of people out of work and affect the community significantly To head off a favorable vote on the formation of a union, Sam, the "heir apparent," wants to start a rumor that formation of a union would force such a move. Either way, looking to the future, he would favor such a move anyhow.		Granting the need for any company to earn a return for its stockholders, the current president, Sam's father, should hold wide discussions with all concerned, including leading community officials & the workers, to assess the situation. Starting a rumor should not take place, but the workers should honestly be made aware of all of the facts. Any decision made should be as fair as possible to both those who brought the company along in the past and to the local community.
(SINCE W) WARRANT		(UNLESS R) REBUTTAL OR EXCEPTION
Decisions by companies (of long standing) in a city to move away from the workers who helped develop them and the communities that helped support them are unfair and do not reflect what postmodern society should be like in the future.		1. The workers do unionize and make most unfair demands on the company that simply cannot be met and still stay in business. 2. Reasonable severance

TEST NO. 1 (KANT)
(consistency)

(ON ACCOUNT OF B)
BACKING

As the world moves into the 21st century, politicians and those who put them in office will need increasingly to enact legislation that initially encourages and then ultimately, if necessary, forces companies to be "good citizens" on a worldwide basis so that workers are treated fairly throughout their entire working careers.

TEST No.2 (MILL)
(net consequences)

packages and early retirement schemes are made available, as well opportunity for those qualified and having an interest to move along with the company.

TEST No. 3
(ARISTOTLE)
(intentions)

Key: Jurisprudential Argument Terms:

D = Data (A statement of a situation that prevails including evidence, elements, sources, samples of facts)
Q = Modal Qualifier (adverbs employed to qualify conclusions based on strength of warrants (e.g., necessarily, probably)
C = Conclusion (claim or conclusion that we wish to establish)
W = Warrant (practical standards or canons of argument designed to provide an answer to the question, "How do you get there?"
B = Backing (categorical statements of fact that lend further support to the bridge-like warrants)
R = Conditions of Exception (arguments of rebuttal or exception that tend to refute or "soften" the strength of the conclusion)

Environmental **Ethical Decision-Making Problems**

Introduction

The third and final category of ethical problems (environmental) contains two case situations in which the individual as a concerned person and an "enlightened world citizen" may wish to, or need to, make a decision of an ethical nature about his or her relationship to the environment. It should be kept in mind that we can delineate here between what might be called the *social* environment and, of course, the *physical* or *natural* environment.

Thus, once again I am agreeing, as I explained above, that all ethical problems are ultimately personal problems (i.e., those problems encountered by a person typically in ethical relationships (1) between himself or herself and other persons at home or in social settings, or (2) with fellow professionals or colleagues (or customers), or (3) with other persons within what might be called the social or physical environment. Accordingly, I chose to make this tripartite subdivision of all possible ethical problems for purposes of ease of understanding and convenience.

The Collision Between Ecology and Capitalism. The influence of ecology began to be felt during the 1970s when some scholars in North American society began to predict the upcoming clash between ecology and traditional economic theory. This influence and the potential collision with capitalism became truly recognizable and significant during the last quarter of the 20th century. It is not unusual that very little attention has been paid to this threatening development by those in the general population earlier. As a matter of fact, the large majority of people still conduct their lives in the 21st century in a manner that clearly indicates they still do not appreciate the gravity of the situation. Maybe people will finally come to their senses when they are finally confronted by the purported Cree Indian prophecy: "When the last tree is cut down, the last fish eaten, and the last stream poisoned, you will realize that you can't eat money." Mark Twain said it even more succinctly: "Humans are the only animals that blush, and need to."

Although this problem has been with us over the centuries, leaders evidently through lack of understanding and appreciation of it, along with the growth of the world's population and related societal development, have never brought the basic issue home to people forcibly. Now the problem is here to stay; so, after having the matter called to my attention a generation ago, I soon decided that it. too, should be considered a persistent problem to my field in the same way as the other five forces of values, politics, nationalism, economics, and religion. No longer, as it has almost always been possible in the past, can we simply move elsewhere to locate another abundant supply of game to hunt, water to drink, or mineral resources to exploit when natural resources are depleted.

Case 5 "Shall I Run for Elective Office?"

Geraldo is the sort of person that everyone likes to "have on their side." He is the proverbial tall, dark, and good-looking fellow, the type who makes a good hero in the movies. Actually he works as a dispatcher in a local trucking firm, having started there after he finished community college with an associate in arts degree. Along the way he was active in several sports, and more recently he has been active in a local theater company. Geraldo is a most personable fellow that everyone seems to like. He is reasonably self-centered, but also shows great interest in other people, their concerns, and the overall community itself. Because the coastal city where he lives in heavily industrialized, recently a number of concerns have been raised about the environment. Geraldo sympathizes with these concerns and has actually made contributions to the efforts of two different groups working to improve the situation. However, as seems to be the case quite often nowadays, the mayor and the city council appear reluctant to rein in those forces that are working to develop enterprises that will undoubtedly make the environmental situation worse. Interestingly, it is fair to say that those behind the aggressive expansion taking place are strong contributors to the campaign funds of the various members of the city council when they run for reelection. All in all, a number of leading citizens are anxious to put at least one voice on the council who will argue for moderation of the onrushing expansion. There really seems to be a dearth of good, "environmentally conscious" candidates who might run. A group that is conscious of this fact meets to discuss a possible candidate to back in the upcoming election. They decide that Geraldo would be just the person to run for one of the two open spots in the council. When asked, the idea appeals to Geraldo initially. But when he thinks about the time that would be involved in an already crowded existence, he can't bring himself to take the step. He reasons that there are many people much better qualified than he is who should stand for election. However, Geraldo needs to come up with a decision that he can live with too.

Analysis. This sample case relates to what I am calling here *social* environmental ethics. (The second sample case involves consideration of *natural* or *physical* environmental ethics.) Of course, in this instance there is no law that says that Geraldo must run for office. He has a right to say "no" to the idea. However, using the three-step approach that we have recommended here--if all of the Geraldos of the world decide that they are just too busy to run for this or that elective office for one or more reasons--the future of democratic societies will soon become precarious. So we certainly don't want to see this type of rejection universalized (Test No. 1), so to speak. Second, the net consequences (Test No. 2) of qualified people typically avoiding their responsibility to serve the community in one or more ways will obviously be that this city will become a less desirable place in which to live. In fact this is exactly what is happening at the various levels but to different degrees all over the country. The best people are not necessarily running for election to the many offices that become open on a regular schedule. The final (third) step that we have recommended to help with an analysis of an ethical situation has to do with Geraldo's intentions (Test No. 3). Is he really too busy at this time to get involved? Does he feel that he doesn't have a duty or responsibility to get involved somehow in helping to make his community a better place? Does he know of some personality or knowledge deficiency that he has which would "disqualify" him from serving well as a member of the city council. Does he not care what happens to the environment of the city?

Table 6
ANALYSIS NO. 5 (CIVIC RESPONSIBILITY)
(For use with Steps One, Two, and Three)

D DATA	Q SO, PROBABLY	C CONCLUSION
Geraldo, an intelligent, conscientious, personable young man, has shown concern for the future of his community and its environment. Those concerned with the overly aggressive expansion have asked Geraldo to stand for election to the city council. He has such a busy life already that he doesn't want to take the time, but he feels a bit guilty.		If he is truly concerned about what is happening to his community and intends to remain there in the future, and there are no extenuating cir--cumstances to prevent him from doing so, Geraldo should probably accept the offer and stand for office.
(SINCE W) WARRANT		UNLESS R) REBUTTAL OR EXCEPTION
Applying the criterion of universality, it is obvious that if all of the "qualified Geraldos"		1. There is some good reason that would prevent him

of the world decide that they are "too busy to run," democracy, as a political movement, will in time be supplanted by some other, form of government

TEST NO. 1 (KANT)
(**consistency**)

(ON ACCOUNT OF B)
BACKING

Democracy, as a form of government, is relatively new on the political scene as compared to monarchy and oligarchy. People all over the world want to have the freedoms that it seems to offer, not to mention its current alliance with capitalism. However, people are not typically accepting the concurrent duties and responsibilities to be involved and offer public service.

TEST NO. 2 (MILL)
(**net consequences**)

Key: Jurisprudential Argument Terms:

D = Data (A statement of a situation that prevails in-
    cluding evidence, elements, sources, samples of facts)
Q = Modal Qualifier (adverbs employed to qualify conclusions
    based on strength of warrants (e.g., necessarily, probably)
C = Conclusion (claim or conclusion that we wish to establish)
W = Warrant (practical standards or canons of argument designed
    to provide an answer to the question, "How do you get there?")
B = Backing (categorical statements of fact that lend further
    support to the bridge-like warrants)
R = Conditions of Exception (arguments of rebuttal or exception
    that tend to refute or "soften" the strength of the conclusion)

from having adequate time to campaign for office and serve if elected.

2. Geraldo decides that there is some other way that he can serve his community more effectively.

3. He knows of some deficiency in his personality or knowledge that would at times prevent him from being an effective contender and and ongoing public servant.

TEST NO. 3
(**ARISTOTLE**)
(**intentions**)

Case 6: "The Right to Bear Arms"

Gordon is a successful businessman who has built a fine life for himself and his family. As he was getting established in his line of work, he met Kate who was the shipping agent for the same company. After a fairly long courtship, they married and now have three children. The oldest is a nine-year old daughter, Gail, who is an outgoing tomboy in all respects. Two boys are seven and five years, respectively. Gordon was a successful athlete in two sports during his schooldays and was also always active in both hunting and fishing dating back to his high school days. Now in his late 30s, he jogs quite regularly to stay fit. As he explains, "I really don't like jogging, but it helps keep me ready for what I really love, hunting and fishing. Kate got involved in these activities at first, but mainly to please Gordon. She and her present circle of women friends have a variety of interests, but typically play tennis in the summer and are curlers in the winter. For several reasons she also has misgivings about Gordon's involvement of their children in his favorite activities. The idea of fishing doesn't bother her very much, except that the two boys don't really know how to swim yet. But she really doesn't think they should get involved with killing birds and animals, nor does she like the idea of having guns around the house (often in drawers or unlocked cabinets). Gordon laughs about her squeamishness while arguing that a knowledge of guns and their proper usage is basic for everyone. A recent hunting trip for bear really got Kate upset. However. Gordon decided that Gail should go along, and he would see to it that she would be absolutely safe. As it happened, the hunters finally cornered a bear that proceeded to climb a tree. So Bob brought Gail in for the kill and allowed her to take the shot that actually killed the bear. Bob's friends agree with his plan to take the bear's head and have it mounted on a plaque to hang in her room. What then happened, it surprised everyone. It was not the fact that the picture taken of Gail standing proudly next to the dead bear was run in the local newspaper, but that CNN picked up the story of a nine-year old girl shooting a bear. They featured it internationally for a day at the end of their 30-minute news segments. Kate was embarrassed and doesn't know what to do--and now she doesn't know what to say to her friends.

Analysis. The second sample case included here can be categorized as one in which the ethical problem relates to what I have called natural or physical environmental ethics. Generally speaking, situations similar to this one abound all over the world. Various species of fauna are being eliminated from existence on a daily basis. Do humans somehow have a right to kill these creatures in the first place just for the thrill and excitement of the hunt? Admittedly we are at the top of the food chain. Secondly, do we have a right to kill animals and birds when they are not needed for food? Hunting harkens back to the days when people killed for food, of course, but for most people in North America that phase of history is long past. So here we are in a situation where Gordon obviously wants to teach his daughter how to shoot and how to hunt--and then to have the animals mounted as trophies. Of course, so long as he has a license to hunt (can the child too?), and it is in the designated season to hunt this particular species of animal, what he is doing is legal. But he and his family should ultimately decide whether they agree that (1) these activities (i.e., hunting with guns) for "sport" should be universalizable (Test No. 1) and (2) that the net consequences (Test No. 2) of having their children involved with guns and hunting are positive and desirable either. Finally, (3) applying the test of intentions (Test No. 3), only Gordon (and Kate too!) are in a position to decide what the long range aims and specific objectives of such activity are in regard to their children's education and the traits which they hope to develop through the experiences they are providing for them.

Table 7
ANALYSIS NO. 2 (ANIMAL WELFARE/ A CHILD AS HUNTER)
(With (a) the Three-Step Approach Superimposed
on (b) the Jurisprudential Argument Layout)

D DATA	Q SO, PRESUMABLY	C CONCLUSION
Gordon and Kate have three children, the oldest (Gail) is nine years old and two sons are younger. Gordon is really into hunting and fishing as hobbies along with an ample supply of guns and fishing equipment. Kate is not pleased with the idea of the children being involved with hunting and having guns around the house. Recently Gordon took Gail along on a hunting trip and allowed her to shoot a treed bear. The mounted head is to be hung in her room.		Kate should confront Gordon in regard to her feelings about the ethics of killing wild anima (and so-called game fish) for so-called sport. She should also discuss gun safety around the house and whether their children should be developing a "gun mentality" as well.

(SINCE W)
WARRANT

It seems cruel enough to slaughter animals, fowl, and fish daily to provide food for a population that is increasing out of control on a closed-system planet, but to do so wantonly in the name of sport is unfair (and often illegal). Also, maintaining a "gun mentality" in the home and community is questionable in a world striving for global peace.

TEST No.1 (KANT)
(consistency)

(ON ACCOUNT OF B)
BACKING

The clash of ecology & economics is continuing unchecked on a planet with finite resources. Species of animals, fowl, and fish are being eliminated forever. In addition to possibly being not ethical, it is also very impractical. The inculcation of a "gun mentality" in a world where peace and the brotherhood of humankind is desired seems to be highly undesirable.

TEST No.2 (MILL)
(net consequences)

Key: Jurisprudential Argument Terms:

D = Data (A statement of a situation that prevails including evidence, elements, sources, samples of facts)

(UNLESS R)
REBUTTAL OR EXCEPTION

1. Gordon and Kate reach consensus on the idea that the creatures of the earth are here for humans' use since the human has been designated by the Creator supreme to all other sentient creatures on earth.

2. Gordon can convince Kate that knowledge of guns for self-defense is essential since the veneer of civilization may crack at any given moment.

3. Gordon & Kate can find agreement on the need for their children to know how to hunt and fish as possible self-preservation competencies when or if the occasion arises.

TEST No. 3
(ARISTOTLE)
(intentions)

Q = Modal Qualifier (adverbs employed to qualify conclusions based on strength of warrants (e.g., necessarily, probably)
C = Conclusion (claim or conclusion that we wish to establish)
W = Warrant (practical standards or canons of argument designed to provide an answer to the question, "How do you get there?"
B = Backing (categorical statements of fact that lend further support to the bridge-like warrants)
R = Conditions of Exception (arguments of rebuttal or exception that tend to refute or "soften" the strength of the conclusion)

Table 8
SAMPLE FORM FOR USE WITH A DECISION-MAKING ANALYSIS

(Name of Case: _____)

D DATA	Q SO, PROBABLY? (NECESSARILY?)	C CONCLUSION
(SINCE W) WARRANT		(UNLESS R) REBUTTAL OR EXCEPTION
		1.
		2.
		3.
TEST No.1 (KANT) (**consistency**)		
		TEST NO. 3 **(ARISTOTLE))** (**intentions**)
(ON ACCOUNT OF B) BACKING		

92

TEST No.2 (MILL)
(net consequences)

Key: Jurisprudential Argument Terms:

D = Data (A statement of a situation that prevails including evidence, elements, sources, samples of facts)
Q = Modal Qualifier (adverbs employed to qualify conclusions based on strength of warrants (e.g., necessarily, probably)
C = Conclusion (claim or conclusion that we wish to establish)
W = Warrant (practical standards or canons of argument designed to provide an answer to the question, "How do you get there?")
B = Backing (categorical statements of fact that lend further support to the bridge-like warrants)
R = Conditions of Exception (arguments of rebuttal exception that tend to refute or "soften" the strength of the conclusion)

SECTION VI
Scientific Ethics:
(The Best Hope for the Future?)

Brief Historical Background

The history of ethics has been characterized by "irregular progress toward complete clarification of each type of ethical judgment" (*Encyclopedia of Philosophy*, III, p. 82). It is obvious that changing political, economic, and other social forces of the various historical periods required the introduction of new ways of conduct, just as today people evidently believe that there is a need for the inclusion of experiences in applied ethics during this transitional period.

Today we are confronted with the basic question: "What are humans?" How do we view human nature? Different views about human nature are what have increased the complexity of the topic at hand. A number of these views are accordingly reflected in the extant approaches to the making of ethical decisions. Stevenson (1987) proposed seven views of human nature for us to consider:

(1) Plato: The Rule of the Wise;
(2) Christianity: God's Salvation;
(3) Marx: Communist Revolution;
(4) Freud: Psychoanalysis;
(5) Sartre: Atheistic Existentialism;
(6) Skinner: The Conditioning of Behavior; and
(7) Lorenz: Innate Aggression.

Obviously, the extent to which one subscribes to one of these views of human nature, or possibly even another extant view, will have an effect on people's ethical decision-making.

Because of changing emphases in "doing" philosophy, until very recently the field of ethics in life generally has been left to theologians, dramatists, novelists. poets, medical doctors, politicians, jurists, scientists, comedians, sport figures, and educational administrators in no special order of importance. These usually well-intentioned people offer a variety of opinions ranging from suggestions to dogma about what is good and bad, right and wrong, about all aspects of life actually.

It does indeed make sense for us to be working toward the elimination of irrational beliefs. At the same time each of us, as a presumably free individual in an evolving society, should attempt to discover the soundest possible approach to ethical decision-making. Recognizing that the task of normative inquiry can be most difficult, I felt a need to justify my own personal theory of ethics that could be applied to both personal and professional living. To me it was readily apparent that an intelligent person should be able to state correctly, elucidate sufficiently, and defend adequately his/her moral or ethical claims and arguments about participation in personal, professional, and "environmental" living.

In Section Two, I explained that people in North America have by and large never specifically learned how to make ethical decisions. I then mentioned that I would be recommending a three-step approach (i.e., from Kant, to Mill, to Aristotle) in Section Four for initial use in any such decision-making. I felt that this "easy-entry" approach was one that could be used *BEFORE* a person makes a final decision based on more experience and further maturation in life.

Even after explaining that daily we typically make ethical decisions that are "personal, professional, and environmental," in Section Three, I did my best to stay as neutral as possible on the topic. I described how the discipline of philosophy had produced six "leading approaches" to ethical decision-making. But then I decided, also, that I had a responsibility to make my own position on ethical decision-making known at some point. I did this because I felt--especially since the turbulent 1960s when most students demanded it as a right--(1) that I owed that to you, and (2) that I had finally decided myself that what has been called "scientific ethics" offers the best hope for the entire world in the 21st century.

Human beings have made at least recognizable progress in their ongoing relationship to the surrounding environment. However, as we enter the 21st century, it is increasingly apparent that, despite the significant lowering of tensions between the two former superpowers, there is still great insecurity in people's attempt to live together constructively and peacefully on our closed planet. I now personally believe that "scientific" ethics offers the best hope in the long range for the future of humankind. So please allow me to repeat why I believe this to be true.

This topic is vital. Recall that in 1965 Burtt wrote that "The greatest danger to his [man's] future lies in the distorting emotions and destructive passions that he has not yet overcome" (p. 311). Looking ahead hopefully, however, he stated that humans did have a capacity for self-understanding. He believed, also, that this therefore offered the possibility of entering the "inclusive universe" with humans striving for freedom and self-fulfillment. Agreeing with this position, I now state my belief that the general adoption of scientific ethics may provide the answer for humans entering this "inclusive universe."

Back in the mid-1970s in North America, a developing awareness of the need for the application of an ethical approach to personal and professional living became apparent from various sources. *The New York Times* reported on Feb. 26, 1978 that "nowadays students in many disciplines are enrolling in new ethics courses in a variety of undergraduate departments and professional schools. . . . part of the impetus for new programs stems from the social consciousness of the 1960s." This social consciousness heightened in the 1980s' decade, so that in 1986 Fox and DeMarco stated,

> For little more than a decade, philosophic ethics has been faced with a relatively new challenge: to provide theoretical frameworks within which practical moral problems can be solved. This challenge has been posed from many quarters, from outside as well as within philosophy (Preface).

Keeping the above in mind, I'll quickly review some earlier thoughts in this book briefly . The term "ethics" is employed typically in three different ways, each of which has a relation to the other, and all of which will be used here. First, it is used to classify a general pattern or "way of life" (e.g., Muslim or Christian ethics). Second, it refers to a listing of rules of conduct, or what is called a moral code (e.g., the "fair play" ethics of an athlete in a particular culture). Last, it has come to be used when describing inquiry about ways of life and rules of conduct (e.g., that subdivision of philosophy known as metaethics).

A Person's Implicit "Sense of Life"

For better or worse, each of us within our individual growth and development patterns have been conditioned by what Rand (1960) called a "psychological recorder"--i.e., the integrating mechanism of a person's subconscious. This so-called "sense of life" is, she said, "a pre-conceptual equivalent of metaphysics, an emotional, subconscious integrated appraisal of man and existence. It sets the nature of a person's emotional response and the essence of that person's character" (p. 31). For better or worse, this child or young person is making choices, forming value judgments, experiencing emotions, and in many,

many ways is acquiring an implicit view of life.

So far so good. My further hope, as a professional interested in education and philosophy, is that all young people will move on from this point to develop their rational powers. In such instances, reason can then act as the "programmer" of the individual's "emotional computer." The possible outcome of this liaison is that the "program" will result in the eventual development of a reasonably logical and rational life philosophy. At all costs we should avoid an adolescent who is "integrating blindly, incongruously, and at random" (1960, p. 33). Thus conceived, the goal of education is an individual whose mind and emotions are in harmony, thereby enabling this person to develop his or her potential and achieve maximum effectiveness in life. To the greatest possible extent, the goal is a mature person whose mind "leads" and whose emotions "follow" any such dictates in social living.

The Selection of One Among Several Approaches To Ethical Decision-Making

For years I have been arguing, for example, that highly competitive sport in the United States was becoming too strong a social influence. This might not be a problem if the positive personal and societal influences emanating from participation as players, coaches, owners, spectators, and administrators were obviously clearly superior to the negative ones. Whatever your opinion on this controversial subject, no one can argue but that young people need help to make intelligent decisions in these areas affecting their lives so strongly. You will recall that in Section Three I identified the major approaches to ethical decision-making as (1) authoritarianism (legalism), (2) relativism (or antinomianism), (3) situationism (with some similarity to #1), (4) scientific ethics (pragmatism applied to ethics), (5) "good reasons" approach (the "moral point of view"), and (6) emotivism (analytic philosophy's response to ethical problems that arise).

A Scientific-Ethics Approach to Ethical Decision-Making

As I mentioned above, I have personally opted for a scientific-ethics approach to ethical decision-making. So my assignment here it to provide an example that outlines how it can work in practice. My initial premise is that we have been living in a crisis of human values during the second half of the twentieth century. We have traditionally turned to religion and philosophy for moral and ethical guidance, but today confidence in these fields has been diminishing. Conversely, many others have found that the invasion of science and technology into our lives has bestowed benefits upon us, but they question at times the "hazardous side effects" of such progress. (Witness the controversy about the possible cloning of human body parts to help those stricken with various debilitating diseases and associated problems.)

We have been told further that the twentieth century was a transitional one in which the old order is most definitely being replaced by the new as the world moves into the 21st century. But what is not generally appreciated is that the rate of change in society is gradually accelerating--and this acceleration may well continue to increase. All of this has led me to align myself ever more strongly with the pragmatic position holding that we in the Western world must eliminate the persisting dualism that has traditionally separated investigation about the physical world from the study of human behavior in relation to moral values and virtues. I have been comforted by the fact that I am far from alone in holding this position. Rorty (1982), for example, explained how the pragmatist holding this stance,

> sees no need to worry about whether Plato or Kant was right in thinking that something nonspatio-temporal made moral judgments true, nor about whether the absence of such a thing means that such judgments are "merely expressions of emotion" or "merely conventional" or "merely subjective" (p. xvi).

It is my position, therefore, that society's present predicament demands more than the application of traditional philosophic or current analytic approaches to solve problems in ethical decision-making. Society has typically drifted and also failed to employ scientific method in the realm of so-called moral goods, as well as in the realm of so-called natural goods. This has kept our world in a position where changes in values have come about accidentally or arbitrarily (or with some combination of the two). Yet social theory has warned us in this respect repeatedly about the powerful controlling influences of societal values and norms.

Accordingly, what is needed is consensus on the idea that there is no inevitable, unassailable difference in kind between what we have called "human nature" and what we have identified as the "physical world." If such consensus could be achieved, we would then be able to bring the forces of science to bear increasingly and more effectively on all human behavior. Actually, John Dewey saw this need when he recommended that the consequences of "inherited institutions and customs" should be examined with an eye to "intelligent consideration of the ways in which they are to be intentionally modified on behalf of generation of different consequences" [what a way with words he didn't have!] (1929, pp. 272-273). Dewey then went one step further with the assertion that we need a faith that (1) science can indeed bring about complete agreement on factual belief about human behavior; (2) such agreement in factual belief will soon result in agreement in attitudes held by people; and (3) resultantly, continuous adaptation of values to society's changing needs will eventually effect the directed reconstruction of all social institutions (1948, p. xxiii).

> **(Note:** If the truth be known, I think this is exactly what has been happening in most of our ethical dilemmas in an agonizingly slow, amorphous way. However, the trouble with permitting such drift is that it often results in a dubious outcome. Eventually, keeping in mind the developments in regard to nuclear armaments and general environmental degradation, this could well mean that we earthlings will destroy ourselves in the process!)

Interestingly, if society were to place its faith in scientific method as described immediately above, it would in no way negate the work of the analytic philosopher who subscribes to the language analysis technique within an emotivist approach. In fact, such analytic endeavor is scientific and can assist science in a vital way by dispensing with possible fallacious premises and "non-sense" terms. This would result in more insightful, correctly stated hypotheses. However, in terms of human behavior, it is at this point that a wholly scientific approach to ethics parts company with emotivism. The problematic factual statements are not automatically referred to the social scientist by the pragmatist, as is the case with the emotivist. Indeed, the distinction between the factual statements and the value statement is not made--it is explicitly rejected!

The classic scientific method itself is brought to bear in problem-solving. Reflective thinking creates the ideas that serve as tentative solutions for concrete problems of all kinds. In the process the person as a problem-solving organism is confronted with a rapidly changing culture and must be prepared therefore to make adjustments. Habitual and/or impulsive response will often not be effective--and certainly not as effective as reflective thinking that employs both the experience of the past and the introduction of creative ideas.

As explained by Albert and others, the criterion of truth is directly related to the outcome of the reflective process. Those ideas which are successful in resolving problematic situations are true, whereas those which do not lead to satisfactory adjustments are false. Truth is relative rather than absolute, changing rather than eternal. In science, ideas function as tentative solutions for concrete problems--i.e., as hypotheses, which must be tested by experiment (1975, p. 282).

What has just been described is, of course, basically a pragmatic idea of knowledge and truth, one that was made available to us by modern scientific development (after Darwin's evolutionary theory). Truth is to be tested (1) by its correspondence with reality and (2) by its practical results. This treatment of knowledge lies between the extremes of reason and sense perception and--in keeping with analytic philosophy's verifiability theory of meaning--revolves about those conditions under which a statement does have meaning, and just what specific meaning in the light of such conditions. Thus, if a proposition truly does have meaning, it must make some difference in people's lives. Viewed in this manner, we can appreciate what James called the "cash value" of an idea--the import that certain knowledge, having served people as an "instrument for verification," has for the fulfillment of human purpose.

The human mind, viewed within the context of pragmatism, is a social phenomenon that "expands" when interactions having meaning occur between organisms because of their identification with each other. In this way the individual's mind serves to form knowledge (or truth) because of the experiences with which it is involved. Such a mind must be adaptable because it encounters novelty in the process of living. The human's relationship with the world is a precarious one within this context. Mind "is an abstraction derived from the concreta of intelligent behavior" (Kaplan, 1961, p. 26). Through a gradual evolution, the human mind has become that part of the whole of a person that enables the man or woman to cope with the surrounding world. Through experience, therefore, the many problems we encounter have been, are, and will--we trust-- be solved. It's an ever-changing world.

Putting this in present context, we encounter various ethical problems in our lives every day. Some are problems of a highly personal nature, while others have more of an interpersonal orientation. Still other ethical problems that arise are more professional in nature because they relate to our chosen professions. We may not even recognize that some of these problems or issues are indeed ethical in nature. Typically, we seem to be resolving any such issue or problem encountered on the basis of (1) authoritarianism, (2) relativism, or (3) perhaps on the basis of what might be called "common sense, cultural utilitarianism." How much better would (could?) it be, however, if we would avail ourselves of the opportunity to expand the mind's potential through the employment of scientific, experimental method to help devise the best solutions for problems of human behavior that arise regularly?

An Example of a Practical Application

The following is an example of a practical application of a scientific (pragmatic) approach to one persistent problem in competitive sport--the Professional-Semiprofessional-Amateur Controversy. (Space does not permit a detailed review of a more complete analysis carried out by the author; see Zeigler, 1978, pp. 35-42.) The steps to be followed are fully characteristic of an experimental problem-solving situation.

1. The smoothness of life's movement or flow is interrupted by an obstacle. This obstacle creates a problem, and the resultant tension must be resolved to allow further movement (progress?) to take place.

   (**Note:** In this case the underlying problem is that the concepts of "work" and "play" have traditionally been strongly dichotomized in North America. Their typical usage is imprecise and muddled. Nowhere is the confusion more evident than when we are discussing to what extent this nomenclature [i.e., work and play] may be applied when referring to the various levels of sport participation. This accentuates what may be called the "Professional-Semiprofessional-Amateur Controversy," a problem that has been with humankind since ancient times.)

2. Humankind marshals all available, pertinent facts to help with the solution of the problem. Data gathered tends to fall in one or more patterns Subsequent analysis offers the possibility of various alternatives for action--one of which should be chosen as a working hypothesis.

   (**Note**: The terms indicated above were:

   (1) Defined carefully initially and then placed in what was called a

traditional play-work definitional diagram as applied to sport and athletics. Differentiation was made among synthetic, analytic, and pseudo-statements.

(2) Then , the status, along with brief historical data,of sport/athletics in North America was reviewed [with primary attention to the university level].

(3) Finally, the possible relationship among the prevailing, pivotal social forces [e.g., economics, nationalism] and the status of sport was discussed. The differences in the interpretation of various concepts in the three leading types of political states [i.e., democratic, communistic, monarchic] were explained. It was explained further why and how the terms "work" and "play" have become so sharply dichotomized. Also, the evident necessity for reevaluation of some of our basic assumptions about the outmoded amateur code in sport was discussed. It was pointed out as well that the professional in sport today is largely being professional in only a limited sense of the word [i.e., concern for money]. Typically, there is no lifetime commitment to serve society through various contributions to one sport in particular, and to all sports in general. The argument was made further that the amateur should be regarded as the beginner--not as the modern Olympic performer who during the 20th century somehow refrained from taking cash on the spot for his performance [but who received all kinds of substantive support along the way].)

Next, as a result of the investigation described above, one working hypothesis among the various courses of action open on the basis of the type of political state operating in North America was selected for experimentation. A taxonomy was devised and is recommended below for consideration and implementation. In this model the concepts of "work" and "play" as aspects of a person's "active occupation" are altered in such a way so as not to present any insurmountable difficulties in evolving democracies. This taxonomy is titled "Aspects of a Person's Active Occupation," with play, art, and work (as defined by Dewey) included as the three appropriate aspects. These terms were interrelated from the standpoint of a concept of the "unified organism." (Figure 1 below.)

(Next page, please)

Figure 1
Aspects of a Person's "Active Occupation"
(1. Play ------- 2. Art ------- 3. Work)

	LEVEL I	LEVEL II	LEVEL III
Goals Continuum		Short Range ------- Middle Range ------Long Range	
Categories of Interest	THE UNIFIED ORGANISM	1. Physical education-recreation interests 2. Social education-recreation interests 3. Learning education-recreation interests 4. Aesthetic education-recreation interests 5. Communicative educ.-recreation interests	
Amateur-Professional Continuum		Amateur ------ Semiprofessional ----Professional	
Freedom-Constraint Continuum		Freedom ------ Limited Freedom ----- Constraint (No Freedom)	

---

3. Obviously, a working hypothesis must be tested to see if the present problem/issue may be solved through the application of the particular hypothesis selected for experimentation. If, after a trial for a reasonable period of time, this hypothesis doesn't seem to be solving the problem, another alternative hypothesis should be tried. An hypothesis that proves to be acceptable provides new information. It thereby becomes true in the sense that it offers a frame of reference for the organizing of facts. Subsequently, this results in a central meaning that may then be called

knowledge.

4. Determination of knowledge based on agreement in factual belief that is communicated to citizens in evolving democracies should soon result in agreement in attitude. Admittedly, social progress in any given area of endeavor is never a "straight-line affair," but continuous adaptation of values to the culture's changing needs will in time effect the directed reconstruction of all social institutions.

It is at this point that pragmatic (experimentalistic) theory of knowledge merges with the value theory of scientific ethics. This can be so inasmuch as such knowledge acquired frees humans to initiate subsequent action furthering the process of movement and change on into the indefinite future (as adapted from Zeigler, 1989, pp. 54 et ff.).

I believe there is logic in a bona fide progression--if (1) the person wishes to progress and (2) is sufficiently capable--through the ranks of the amateur athlete to that of the semiprofessional, and finally to that of the highly trained, proficient athletic performer--a professional (in all the best senses of this term, we hope). Based on the model described above (Figure 1), if a boy plays baseball after school, his goals are short range and therefore conceived as "play." If he continues with his interest in high school and university, and were to receive an athletic scholarship to attend university, play might soon take on many of the aspects of work. Further, when this young man (or a woman in one of a number of sports) goes away to university on a baseball scholarship, he may then be considered semiprofessional (a semipro). This would be so (1) because of the time being spent, (2) because of the middle range goals attendant to his athletic activity, (3) because of the level of performance he has achieved, and (4) because he is being paid for performing the baseball skills he has mastered. If the young man is then chosen in a draft by the major leagues, he will be forced to make a decision at Level II, the Goals Continuum, and also at the Level III continuum about moving from the Semiprofessional stage to the Professional stage. If the athlete succeeds at this point, he has moved to status as a Professional so long as he continues to maintain a high level of performance.

Summary

Although it has undoubtedly been said many times before, these do appear to be truly unusual times. A world transformation is occurring, and such change is coming about rapidly because the tempo of civilization appears to be increasing exponentially. We are told that behavioral science, along with natural science, is leading humans to believe that many of their problems are as much structural as they are ideological. In other words, disregarding whether a political or social solution is to "the right" or "the left," we need to move forward to improve the world situation for our descendants. It is this type of reasoning that rekindled my interest in the elimination of the long-standing distinction between what have been called moral goods and natural goods.

We are being urged further to prepare for a continuing technological thrust. This means that we will necessarily have to recognize changing values with their accompanying language concomitants. In a way we are searching for an ethic in a new culture that has not yet arrived! All of these changes are having their inevitable effect on competitive sport (as one example of a changing social institution). As the reader reflects on the example provided here in Figure 1 to discuss the viability of a pragmatic, scientific-ethics approach that might assist with the problem in professional, semiprofessional, and amateur sport we are facing, think about how ridiculous the selection process in connection with the assembly of the men's Olympic basketball team of the United States became when amateurism "went out the window." And so I say, "Avery Brundage [the longtime president of the International Olympic Committee] stop spinning in your grave. There is nothing you can do about the fact that the United States team is being made up of basketball players who are all millionaires in their own right because of their athletic talent."

But is this development so wrong or evil? Not necessarily; but I do believe it is wrong at this moment because we have drifted into it with inadequate rationalization. The U.S.A. lost the gold medal in 1988, and then was determined to win it back in Barcelona in 1992. The team did win and the "flood gates" have been open to confirmed professionals ever since. The United States Olympic Committee has certified the selection process for squad members. And, as we know, the International Olympic Committee permits all national committees to make such decisions about eligibility. However, we could have prevented this farce. Indeed, we might have been able to rationalize this situation adequately and properly with sufficient advance planning and solicitation of world approval for this transition to out-and-out professionalism in

Olympic sport.

    Finally, my general conclusion is that the pragmatic, scientific-ethics approach, embodying also careful application of language analysis at all appropriate points, offers the best and ultimately the most humane approach to the many problematic issues our culture is now facing. We cannot escape the evidence that new, continually changing values are transforming our culture. Whether we are facing ethical decisions in our home life, our professional endeavor, or in our competitive sport and other recreational pursuits, this scientific-method approach offers humankind not a philosophy of life, but an explicit approach to applied philosophical understanding. This will evolve steadily as a philosophy for the living of life today and tomorrow.

SECTION SEVEN
Looking to the Future

Look not mournfully to the past--it comes not back again;
wisely improve the present--it is thine; go forth to meet
the shadowy future without fear, and with a manly heart.
                    --Longfellow

This is not a very happy time in the history of the world. As someone in his eighties, I confess that I am disappointed that the world isn't in better shape to face the 21st century. Somehow I had foolishly assumed that the affairs of humankind would improve considerably during the course of my life on earth. Well, they have in a number of ways, I suppose, but human beings still face an unbelievably complex task as they face the future. We need to work carefully and systematically to improve the physical condition of the planet Earth--if it isn't already too late.

How We Might Improve the Planet

Although the large majority of us wish that peace, happiness, harmony, and well-being could prevail globally, such has not happened. Prospects for such a happy state of affairs don't seem very likely in the foreseeable future either. Thus, to start with, I am inclined to wish forlornly that all of the clashing religious opinions and beliefs based on hoary tradition would silently go away. Then maybe prevailing world conditions would somehow begin to improve.

But this is wishful thinking unless improved institutions are created to take their place and make the entire world a better place in which to live. (Note here that I am recognizing the perennial designation of Canada--with all of its problems!--as one of the "best countries" in the world in which to live. Certainly I, for one, am not complaining--that's for certain!)

At this point I am anxious to convey the thought that it will only be through positive meliorism, philosophically speaking, that we humans will be able to do something to improve the prevailing disturbing, highly perplexing, and frustrating plight of the world as it struggles in the now (so tritely named) global village.

Implementing what is known as philosophical meliorism means simply that men and women working together in a spirit of brotherhood and sisterhood must work positively, not negatively, to make this "global ballgame" live up to the letter and spirit of the rules that are established by the U.N. and affiliated organizations. (As a former coach, I just had to throw in that 'sport speak' terminology.)

I believe that, in the absence of a sign from on high, we simply must--by ourselves (!)--dredge up the apocalypse (or unveiling) of the ethical core present in all world religions pointing to "a fuller understanding of the oneness of humankind." This we had better do very, very soon. In fact we need to do this by devising institutions that improve on these present outdated relics known as "time-proven" religions.

I say this because I am inclined to believe that the achievement for "good" of many of these theistic and/or spiritualistic approaches may soon be exceeded by their negative "bads" as their proponents parry and thrust repeatedly at their presumed arch-enemies and protagonists. (Speak to Mr. Rushdie and the many other religious and political outcasts around the world on this topic.)

So what I have to offer is not "yet another contemporary version of the now endlessly repeated moral counsels of despair," As I see it, positive meliorism (or working collectively to improve life) on the part of people of goodwill all over the world is the only way of salvation offered to us fallible humans in the absence of reasonable evidence that there is indeed a "Messianic vision" at the core of the 13 more or less established world religions.

How did I arrive at this position as my personal response to the persistent or perennial problems faced by humankind (i.e., war, famine, death, and pestilence)? As a young person, I soon realized the inherent limitations of a religious faith to which I was almost automatically bound by reason of birth. Instead of having some conception of theism of dubious historical origin foisted upon him or her in youth, my contention is that each young person should be encouraged by his or her parents to work this philosophic/religious problem out for himself or herself through careful reflection while growing to maturity. I believe that an individual's development and tentative "solution" about such matters would then have a deeper, more meaningful influence on the subsequent development of this individual as a socially oriented person, as well as a rational professional or tradesperson in an increasing complex and changing social environment.

Having personally been raised in a largely Judeo-Christian culture carried along by onrushing science and technology, I could not help but challenge what I perceived to be the inherent weaknesses of blind faith presented by fallible humans masking (literally) in the robes of this organized religion. In the process, what I thought I had learned from philosophers in my earlier days is also not being received with anywhere nearly the same authority as previously. Philosophers today, largely because of a truncated approach to their task, rarely speak to the larger questions of life and living.

So I soon came to accept a broader definition of religion, one conceived as "the pursuit of that which an educated and presumably enlightened person regards as most worthy and important in life." What I found to be most worthy was the advancement of knowledge for the betterment of humankind along with related teaching and professional service. This to me truly represented a personal challenge, and I reasoned that what I came up with should be fully worthy of a person's complete devotion.

Moreover, our culture has now become increasingly multiethnic and is resultantly characterized by the faiths and religious positions of all of these migrating peoples. I do respect the personal religious stances taken by many, but one soon comprehends that no one of the approximately 13 historical faiths has a corner on the market of religious truth. This situation has indeed created a highly confusing ethical "miasma," a situation where presently the thoughts of politicians, the writings of novelists, and the jibes of comedians seemed to be taking over on the subject of human values. Fortunately, however, there is a large amount of room for agreement among people of good will regardless of which faith or creed to which they subscribe. This would also be true for those who have never been involved, or are no longer involved, with some organized form of belief.

For example, I felt that we could agree that the cosmos as we know it is evolving or developing in time. It was obvious to me, also, that the mystery of this universe has already become a highly effective source of awe and reverence for many humans. Additionally, I could see as a developing young person that our growing knowledge of this vast cosmos was becoming increasingly valuable in helping us to guide our lives in an improved manner. Further, although some would debate this point, there is evidence of a type of progress through both inorganic and biological evolution.

Naively I had supposed that the world situation would improve markedly in my lifetime in the 20th century. Well, it has, and it hasn't. Fortunately, humankind is now beginning to realize that it has certain responsibilities, and accompanying powers, for the continuation of this evolution. We are gradually understanding further that the practical application of universal brotherhood, undivided by nation, race, or creed, is vital if humankind wishes to survive. Whether we can progress as we hope to do in human affairs is a moot question.

The world is beginning to understand further that a form of democratic process in human relations provides the best opportunity for a person to develop to the maximum of his or her potentialities. Additionally, we are also steadily increasing worldwide awareness that the development of any one person shall not be at the expense of the group or society at large.

As defined above, I believe that philosophic/religious growth should be basic to all human life. It is an attitude of mind and "spirit" which should permeate all aspects of human endeavor. It is challenging to us that life as we know it in this universe appears to be characterized by creativity. Thus, it is reasonable to argue that the purpose of religion is to assist with the integration of all of a person's behavior with this presumed creativity within the universe. If religion is defined broadly, we may state that a critical and developing reason is a powerful aid in the search for a logically valid religious position.

I find that I want each individual to be free to seek philosophic/religious "truth" unhampered by official creed or outdated religious dogmas. Young people in schools and university should have an opportunity to study all of the world's great religions comparatively. In this way they will remain receptive to religious truth wherever it may be found.

I argue further that most--if not all!--aspects of life are (potentially) accessible to scientific study. This fact can be of enormous significance in the centuries that lie ahead. As the body of scientific knowledge grows, this will help to develop attitudes (as defined in psychology) that could lead to enlightened social action. Ultimately, to me this is a much truer criterion of the religious quality of a person's life than any religious ideas which are dutifully professed rote as part of a Sunday ritual.

As I see it, also, it is axiomatic that the church and the state should remain separate. Nevertheless, I do understand that it is most important for members of any religious group--*acting as individuals*--to take responsibility for positive social action. All enlightened citizens should be involved in the political process at some level.

This leads me finally to the conclusion that the hoary religious "truths" of the past are truly devoid of meaning for people facing the world of the 21st century. Some humanities scholars may believe, for example, that the "utopian speculation of the human imagination which constitutes the core of the liberal arts" is indeed a "moral counsel of despair" unless we all have "an encounter with a reality larger than the one we ourselves invent" (R. Woodman, The Univ. of Western Ontario). If Professor Woodman has had this "encounter," I am glad for him. However, I am finding that the Pennsylvania "Dutch" motto is creeping up on me fast. I am growing "too soon oldt und too late schmart." Thus, I am terribly worried about the future, an indeterminate period ahead about which we need to achieve a "Scotch Verdict."

Achieving a "Scotch Verdict" About the Future

Of course, the world must move into the future strongly and boldly, but it will also have to proceed with great care and concern. This is why I think we need to achieve a "Scotch Verdict" about the future.

"Getting in league with the future" or "future forecasting" can be carried out best by making a sincere, solid effort to understand what futuristics or futurology is all about. One could take the next step and apply these findings to one or more aspects of our lives. In *Visions of the Future*, a publication of the well-known Hudson Institute, we are urged to tailor our thinking to three ways of looking at the future: (1) the possible future, (2) the probable future, and (3) the preferable future.

As you might imagine, the possible future includes everything that could happen, and thus perceptions of the future must be formed by us individually and collectively. The probable future refers to occurrences that are likely to happen, and so here the range of alternatives must be considered. Finally, the preferable future relates to an approach whereby people make choices, thereby indicating how they would like things to happen. Underlying all of this are certain basic assumptions or premises such as

(1) that the future hasn't been predetermined by some force or power;

(2) that the future cannot be accurately predicted because we don't understand the process of change that fully; and
(3) that the future will undoubtedly be influenced by choices that people make, but won't necessarily turn out the way they want it to be (Amara, 1981).

As we all appreciate, people have been predicting the future for thousands of years, undoubtedly with a limited degree of success. Considerable headway has been made, of course, since the time when animal entrails were examined to provide insight about the future (one of the techniques of so-called divination). Nowadays, for example, methods of prediction include forecasting by the use of trends and statistics.

John Naisbitt and The Naisbitt Group stated in the first *Megatrends* volume (1982) that "the most reliable way to anticipate the future is by understanding the present." Hence they monitor occurrences all over the world through a technique of descriptive method known as content analysis. They actually monitor the amount of space given to various topics in newspapers--an approach they feel is valid because "the news-reporting process is forced choice in a closed system."

Melnick and associates, in *Visions of the Future,* discuss another aspect of futuristics: the question of "levels of certainty." They explain that the late Herman Kahn, an expert in this area, often used the term "Scotch Verdict" when he was concerned about the level of certainty available prior to making a decision. This idea was borrowed from the Scottish system of justice in which a person charged with the commission of a crime can be found "guilty," "not guilty," or "not been proven guilty." This "not been proven guilty" (or "Scotch") verdict implies there is probably enough evidence to demonstrate that the person charged could be guilty, but that insufficient evidence has been presented to end all reasonable doubt about the matter.

With this continuum that has been developed, at one end we can state we are 100% sure that such-and-such is not true. Accordingly, at the other end of the continuum we can state we are 100% sure that such-and-such is the case. Obviously, in-between these two extremes are gradations of the level of certainty. From here this idea has been carried over to the realm of future forecasting.

There is good reason to believe that we are not considering sufficiently the "Great Transition" that humankind has been experiencing, how there has been a pre-industrial stage, an industrial stage and, finally, a postindustrial stage that has evidently arrived in North America first. Each of the stages has its characteristics that must be recognized. For example, in pre-industrial society there was slow population growth, people lived simply with very little money, and the forces of nature made life very difficult. When the industrial stage or so-called modernization entered the picture, population growth was rapid, wealth increased enormously, and people became increasingly less vulnerable to the destructive forces of nature.

The assumption in so-called modern society is that comprehension of the transition that is occurring can give us some insight as to what the future might hold--not that we can be "100% sure," but at least we might be able to achieve a "Scotch Verdict." If North America is that part of the world that is the most economically and technologically advanced, and as a result completed the Great Transition by becoming a postindustrial culture first, we must be aware of what this will mean to our society. Thus, some argue that we have probably already entered a "super-industrial period" of the Industrial Stage in which "projects will be very large scale; services will be readily available, efficient and sophisticated; people will have vastly increased leisure time; and many new technologies will be created."

It is important that we understand what is happening as we move further forward into what presumably is the final or third stage of the Great Transition. It should be made clear that the level of certainty here in regard to predictions is at Kahn's "Scotch Verdict" point on the continuum. The world has never faced this situation before; so, we don't know exactly how to date the beginning of such a stage. Nevertheless, it seems to be taking place right now with the super-industrial period having started after World War II. As predicted, those developments mentioned above (e.g., services readily available) appear to be continuing.

Some postulate that the rate of population growth is slower than it was 20 years ago; yet, it is also true that people are living longer. Next it is estimated that a greater interdependence among nations and the steady development of new technologies will contribute to a steadily improving economic climate for underdeveloped nations. Finally, it is forecast that advances in science and accompanying technology will bring almost innumerable technologies to the fore that will affect life styles immeasurably all over the world.

This discussion could continue indefinitely, but the important points to be made here are emerging rapidly. First, we need a different way of looking at the subject of so-called natural resources. In this interdependent world, this "global village" if you will, natural resources are more than just the sum of raw materials. They include also the application of technology, the organizational bureaucracy to cope with the materials, and the resultant usefulness of the resource that creates supply and demand. The point seems to be that the total resource picture (as explained here) is reasonably optimistic if correct decisions are made about raw materials, energy, food production, and use of the environment. These are admittedly rather large "IFS".

Finally in "forecasting the future," the need to understand global problems of two types should be stressed. One group is called "mostly understandable problems," and they are solvable. Here reference is made to:

(1) population growth,
(2) natural resource issues,
(3) acceptable environmental health,
(4) shift in society's economic base to service occupations, and
(5) effect of advanced technology.

However, it is the second group classified as "mostly uncertain problems," and these are the problems that could bring on disaster.

First, the Great Transition is affecting the entire world, and the eventual outcome of this new type of cultural change is uncertain. Thus we must be ready for these developments attitudinally.

Second, in this period of changing values and attitudes, people in the various countries and cultures have much to learn, and they will have to make great adjustments as well.

Third, there is the danger that society will--possibly unwittingly--stumble into some irreversible environmental catastrophe (e.g., upper-atmosphere ozone depletion).

Fourth, the whole problem of weapons, wars, and terrorism, and whether the world will be able to stave off all-out nuclear warfare, and

Fifth, and finally, whether bad luck and bad management will somehow block the entire world from undergoing the Great Transition successfully--obviously a great argument for the development of management art and science.

A Final "Playback"

Finally, I asked myself what my efforts all boil down to in the final analysis. I can only repeat that I believe that there is indeed a "crisis in human values" as we move into the 21st century. So I simply repeat that such has created an ethical decision-making dilemma for us all.

In my recent books, *Who Knows What's Right Anymore?* and *Whatever Happened to the Good Life?*, both published by Trafford in 2002, I strove to get at this present crisis in human values in different ways. Here I argue basically again that, for several reasons, the child and adolescent in society today are missing out almost completely on a sound "experiential" introduction to ethics and morality.

This lack is true whether we are referring to that which typically takes place in the home, the school system, or the church--actually an experience that doesn't occur adequately!. In fact, the truth is that typically no systematic instruction in this most important subject is offered at any time. Frankly, I refuse to accept the often-heard "osmosis stance"--i.e., that such knowledge is "better caught than taught!".

Initially I explained how this all came about, how and why such a terrible gap exists. Where previously, for many at least, at least a relatively strong, orthodox, religious indoctrination prevailed. Today I feel such indoctrination as may still exist is most inadequate and is steadily declining as well. This is not necessarily a bad thing in one respect, because these institutions have not kept up with the times because of the "built-in" rigidity of their doctrines. Moreover, the situation has steadily changed in our present multiethnic, secular culture to a point where "confusion reigns" as to ethical conduct. (***If these institutions don't adjust, they should be replaced.***)

First I assessed the North American situation in what has been called the postmodern age. I believe that Americans, and many Canadians as well, do not fully comprehend their unique position in the history of the world's development. In all probability this status will change radically in the 21st century. For that matter. I believe that the years ahead are going to be really difficult and trying for all of the world's citizens.

The United States, as the one major nuclear power, has deliberately assumed the ongoing, overriding task of maintaining large-scale peace. This will be increasingly difficult because a variety of countries, both large and small, may already have, or may soon have, nuclear arms capability. That is one stark fact what makes the future so worrisome.

After discussing the North American situation in the postmodern age, I offered an explanation of the "ethical gap" that exists insofar as people's understanding of ethical decision-making is concerned. I described how we are called upon daily for ethical opinions and/or decision about personal, professional, and environmental (societal) problems. In this connection a person's ethical involvement should be an implicit/explicit experiential approach that necessarily moves daily from one to the other of the three categories mentioned (e.g., personal). At this point, mostly in chart form, I offered a quick look at six of the major ethical routes or approaches extant as offered by the field of philosophy as solutions to today's confusing Western-world scenario.

I have observed that most books of this nature propose what amounts to one specific philosophical, religious, or commonsense stance. However, I do believe fervently that the reader must ultimately make his or her own personal decision about which approach to follow. Thus, I want this to be one that is determined by the individual when "the age of reason" is achieved (let us say, after age 13).

I decided therefore to offer an "easy-entry" approach, a three-step one that can be used safely before a person makes a final decision as to which ethical decision-making approach to follow as more experience and maturation is obtained during life. (Admittedly, many people may never proceed beyond this initial stage--if they get this far!) Fortunately, this three-step approach can be checked or vetted to a degree by superimposing it (actually!) on top of the format in which the law-court argument is explained.

I then decided also that I had a basic responsibility to make my own position on ethical decision-making known clearly. It is what has been called "scientific ethics." I believe it offers the best hope for the entire world in the 21st century. Even though definitive scientific evidence is often not immediately available, I have personally accepted this approach for use immediately after I have carried out the initial three-step scanning of the situation at hand.

So there it is. I offer it to you as one way out of the "ethical confusion" that exists in our madcap, multicultural North America. I hope it helps.

References & Bibliography

Abelson, R., & Friquegnon, M. (1975). *Ethics for modern life.* NY: St. Martin's.
Annas, J. (1981). An *introduction to Plato's Republic.* Oxford: Clarendon.
Anderson, T.C. (1979). *The foundation and structure of Sartrean ethics.* Lawrence, KS: State Regents Press.
Aristotle. *Nicomachean Ethics* (Book III, Chapter 1). In Loomis, L.R. (Ed.). (1943). NY: W.J. Black. (Transl. by J.E.C. Welldon).
Ayer, A.J. (1946). *Language, truth, and logic.* (Rev. Ed.). NY: Dover.

Baier, K. (1970). *The moral point of view.* Ithaca, NY: Cornell University Press.
Baker, R. (1976). Good bad sports. *The New York Times Magazine,* Feb. 1.
Berelson, B. & Steiner, G.A. (1964). *Human behavior: An Inventory of Scientific Finding*s. NY: Harcourt-Brace.
Berger, F. (1984). *Happiness, justice, and freedom: The moral and political philosophy of John Stuart Mill.* Berkeley: Univ. of California.
de Beauvoir, S. (1964). *The ethics of ambiguity.* NY: The Citadel Press.
Blumenthal, W.M. (1977). Business morality has not deteriorated--society has changed. *The New York Times,* Jan. 9.
Bok, D.C. (1975). Can ethics be taught? *Change,* 8, 9:26-30.
Brubacher, J. S. (1978). *On the philosophy of higher education.* San Francisco: Jossey-Bass Publishers.
Burtt, E.A. (1965). *In search of philosophical understanding.* NY: New American Library.

Chace, J. (1977). How "moral" can we get? *The New York Times Magazine,* May 22.
Cogley, J. (July/August, 1972). The storm before the calm. *The Center Magazine* V (4), 2-3.
Coles, R. (1997). *The moral intelligence of children.* NY: Random House.
Commager, H. S. (August 27, 1976) The nature of academic freedom. *Saturday Review,* 13-15, 37.
Csikszentmihalyi, M. (1993). *The evolving self.* New York: HarperCollins.

Denise, T.C., & Peterfreund, S.P. (1992). *Great traditions in ethics.* (7th Ed.). Belmont, CA: Wadsworth.
Dennis, Ann B. (1975). A code of ethics for sociologists and anthropologists? *Social Sciences in Canada,* 3(1-2):14-16.
Dewey, J. (1929), *The quest for certainty.* NY: Minton, Balch & Co.
Dewey, J. & Tufts, J.H. (Eds.). (1932). *Ethics.* (Rev. Ed.). NY: Holt, Rinehart & Winston.
Dewey, J. (1946). *Problems of men.* NY: Henry Holt.
Dewey, J. (1948). *Reconstruction in philosophy.* (Enl. & Upd. Ed.). Boston: The Beacon Press.

Encyclopedia of Philosophy, The (8 vols.) (P. Edwards, Ed.). (1967). NY: Macmillan and The Free Press.
Etzioni, A. (1976). Do as I say, not as I do. *The New York Times Magazine,* Sept. 26.

Fairlie, H. (1978). *The seven deadly sins today.* Washington, DC: New Republic.
Fletcher, J. (1966). *Situation ethics: The new morality.* Philadelphia: The Westminster Press.
Fox, R.M. & DeMarco, J.P. (1990). *Moral reasoning: A philosophic approach to applied ethic*s. Ft. Worth. TX: Holt, Rinehart & Winston.
Fromm, E. (1967). *Man for himself.* NY: Fawcett World Library.

Gardner, P. (1988). *Kierkegaard.* Oxford: Oxford Univ. Press
Goldman, D. (1995). *Emotional intelligence.* NY: Bantam.
Gouinlock, J. (1972). *John Dewey's philosophy of values.* NY: Humanities Press.

Hardie, W. (1980). *Aristotle's ethical theory.* NY: Oxford.
Hawley, A.H. (1986). *Human ecology: A theoretical essay.* Chicago: The University of Chicago Press.
Hayman, R. (1982). *Nietzsche, a critical life.* NY: Penguin.
Hazard, G.C., Jr. (1978). Capitalist ethics. *Yale Alumni Magazine & Journal,* XLI, 8:50-51.
Hechinger, F.M. (1974). Whatever became of sin? *Saturday Review/World,* Sept. 24.
Hibler, R. (1982). *Happiness through tranquility: The school of Epicurus.* Lanham: Univ. Press of America.
Hospers, J. (1953). *An introduction to philosophical analysis.* Englewood Cliffs, NJ: Prentice-Hall. (See, also, 2nd Ed., 1967.)
Huxley, J. (1963). *The politics of ecology.* Santa Barbara, CA: Center for the Study of Democratic Institutions.

Johnson, H.M. (1969). The relevance of the theory of action to historians. *Social Science Quarterly,* 2:46-68.

Kalish, D. & Montague, R. (1964). *Logic: Techniques of formal reasoning.* NY: Harcourt, Brace, & World.
Kant, I. (1938). *Fundamental principles of the metaphysics of ethics.* NY: D. Appleton-Century.

(Transl. by G. Manthey-Zorn).
Kaplan, A. (1961). *The new world of philosophy*. NY: Random House.
Kaufmann, W. (1973). *Without guilt and justice: From decidophobia to autonomy*. NY: Peter H. Wyden.
Kekes, J. (Jan. 1987). Is our morality disintegrating? *Public Affairs Quarterly*, 1, 1:79-94.
Kunz, R.F. (Jan. 2, 1971). An environmental glossary. *Saturday Review*, 67.

Mackie, J. (1980). *Hume's moral theory*. London: Routledge & Kegan Paul.
Maeroff, G.I. (1976). West Point cheaters have a lot of company. *The New York Times*, June 20.
Martin, R. (1985). *Rawls and rights*. Lawrence, KS: Univ. of Kansas Press.
Martens, R. (1976). Kid sports: A den of iniquity or land of promise? *Proceedings of the 79th Annual Meeting, NCPEAM* (Gedvilas, L.L., Ed.). Chicago, IL: Univ. of Illinois, Chicago.
McLellan, D. (1975). *Karl Marx*. NY: Viking.
Mergen, F. (May 1970). Man and his environment. *Yale Magazine*, XXXIII(8): 36-37.
Mill, J.S. *Utilitarianism* (V), 1861.
Moore, G.E. (1948). *Principia ethica*. NY: Cambridge University Press.
Morris, V.C. (1956). Physical education and the philosophy of education. *Journal of HPER*, 27(3), 21-22, 30-31.
Murray, B.G., Jr. (Dec. 10, 1972). What the ecologists can teach the economists. *The New York Times Magazine:* 38-39, 64-65, 70, 72.

National Geographic Society, The. (1970). *How man pollutes his world*. Washington, DC: The Society. (This is an explanatory chart.)
Nell, O. (1975). *Acting on principle: An essay on Kantian ethics*. NY: Columbia University.
New York Times, The (1970). Foul air poses health threat to east, May 1.
New York Times, The. (1976). The growing dishonesty in sports: Is it just a reflection of our American society? Nov. 7.
New York Times, The. (1978). The ethical imperative, in News of the Week in Review, Feb. 26.
Northrop, F.S.C. (1946). *The meeting of East and West*. NY: Macmillan.
Nowell-Smith, P.H. (1954). *Ethics*. Harmondsworth, England.

Plato. Gorgias. In Magill, F.N. (Ed.). (1961). *Masterpieces of world philosophy*. NY: Harper & Row.

Rand, A. (1960). *The romantic manifesto*. NY & Cleveland: World.
Rawls, J. (1971). *A theory of justice*. Cambridge, MA: Harvard University Press.
Redpath, P. (1983). *The moral wisdom of St. Thomas*. Lanham: Univ. Press of America.
Rolston, H. (Jan. 1975). Is there an ecological ethic? *Ethics*, 85(2): 93-109.
Rorty, R. (1982) Philosophy in America today. In *Consequences of Pragmatism (Essays: 1972-1980)* (pp. 211-230. Minneapolis, MN: Univ. of Minnesota Press.
Rorty, R. (1982). Consequences of pragmatism. Minneapolis, MN: University of Minnesota Press.

Saturday Review. (1975). Watergating on main street. (Special Report), 3, 3:10-28.
Saturday Review. (1977). God and science--new allies in the search for values. (Special Report), 5, 12:8-22.
Sears, P. (1969). The steady state: Physical law and moral choice. In P. Shephard & D. McKinley, eds., *The subversive science*. Boston: Houghton Mifflin.
Shils, E. (1983). *The academic ethic*. Chicago: The University of Chicago Press.
Sidgwick, H. *Outline of the history of ethics*. London: Macmillan Ltd. (Published originally in 1886).
Smart, J.J.C. (1986). Utilitarianism and its applications. In J.P. DeMarco & R.M. Fox (Eds.), *New directions in ethics* (pp. 24-41). New York and London: Routledge & Kegan, Paul.
Smith, G.L.C. (Jan. 1, 1971). The ecologist at bay. *Saturday Review*, 68-69.
Smith, J.E. (1982) The need for a recovery of philosophy. *Proceedings of the Seventy-Eighth Meeting of the American Philosophical Association*, 56, 5-18.
Starker, S. (1981). *Epistemology and ethics of G.E. Moore, a critical evaluation*. NY: Humanities Press.
Stevenson, C.L. (1947-48). The nature of ethical disagreement. *Sigma*, 1-2, 8-9.
Stevenson, L. (1987). *Seven theories of human nature*. NY: Oxford University Press.

Titus, H.H. & Keaton, M. (1973). *Ethics for today*. (5th Ed.). NY: D. Van Nostrand.
Toulmin, S. (1964). *The uses of argument*. NY: Cambridge University Press.

Urmson, J.O. (1968). *The emotive theory of ethics*. London: Hutchinson.
Warnock, M. (1966). *Ethics since 1900*. NY: Oxford.

Wright, R. (1994) *The moral animal*. NY: Pantheon.

Zeigler, E.F. (1978). Basic considerations about a philosophy of sport (and its possible relationship with success in competitive sport). *Can. Journal of Applied Sport Sciences*, 3, 1 (March), 35-42.

Zeigler, E. F. (1982). *Decision-making in physical education and athletics administration: A case method approach*. Champaign, IL: Stipes.

Zeigler, E.F. (1984). *Ethics and morality in sport and physical education: An experiential approach*. Champaign, IL: Stipes.

Zeigler, E.F. (1988). Application of a scientific ethics approach to sport decisions. In P.J. Galasso (Ed.), *Philosophy of sport and physical activity* (pp. 303-319). Toronto: Canadian Scholar's Press.

Zeigler, E.F. (1989). *Introduction to sport and physical education philosophy*. Carmel, IN: Benchmark.

Zeigler, E. F. (2002). Who knows what's right anymore? (A Guide to Personal Decision-Making). Victoria, BC: Trafford.

Zeigler, E/F/ (2002). Whatever happened to "the good life?" (or Assessing your "RQ" (recreation quotient). Victoria, BC: Trafford.

ISBN 141202274-6